Mindszenty the Man

Mindszenty the MAN

by
Joseph Vecsey
as told to
Phyllis Schlafly

CARDINAL MINDSZENTY FOUNDATION
ST. LOUIS

The publisher expresses its appreciation to Mr. James Likoudis, of Catholics United for the Faith, for his valuable assistance in surmounting the language barrier.

Cover design by Shirley Starbuck

The picture on the cover shows a beautiful grain called árvalányhaj which grows only on the plains of Hungary. It is a legendary symbol of liberty used by the Hungarian Boy Scouts, set in the Scout insignia with the famous Crown of St. Stephen in the center.

The picture of Cardinal Mindszenty used in the frontispiece was taken in his office in Vienna in 1972. The picture on the back cover shows Cardinal Mindszenty and Phyllis Schlafly in Vienna, November 20, 1971.

Library of Congress Catalog Card Number 72-93906

Published by the Cardinal Mindszenty Foundation
P. O. Box 11321
St. Louis, Missouri 63105

Printed in the United States of America

Table of Contents

Why This Book Was Written

THE CRYING NEED of our times is for noble leaders — for men and women who have the courage to stand fast against false propaganda, who persevere in their principles when they reach high positions, who remain loyal to the people who look up to them, who cannot be seduced by money or scared by power, who listen to the voice of conscience instead of the roar of the crowd, and who are willing to pay the price that leadership demands in terms of self-discipline and difficult decisions.

Great leaders are not usually appointed to their leadership role by a special messenger from God or by the good fortune of a distinguished birth. A Joan of Arc who has visions and hears voices which motivate her to lead in battle is a rarity in history. Most great leaders are ordinary, uninspired people who have made the decision within themselves (1) to accept the responsibilities of leadership, and (2) to pay the painful price that leadership demands. For most people, the responsibility is too heavy a burden and the price of discipline and perseverance is too high.

The last several decades have been singularly lacking in enough nobly-dedicated leaders on all levels to defend the ramparts of civilization against the enemies of freedom and religion. When we get too close to the famous and rich and powerful, we find that most of them have feet of clay. The glitter of their high office is all rubbed off by "inside stories" written by their secretaries or servants or confidants or ghost writers. Never has it been so true that "no man is a hero to his valet."

If we are to cultivate leaders to cope with our current crisis, we must know what kind of soil they sprout in, and what kind of climate will help them grow. Does a clergyman or rabbi want to lead his flock? Does a public official want to lead his or her country, city, or party? Does any man or woman want to lead a worthwhile organization? The same principles of leadership apply in every endeavor. So we must study the ideals, the training, the work habits, the rules of conduct, and the private lives of the few authentic heroes of our times.

By any standard, Cardinal Mindszenty is a leader. He has accepted the responsibilities of leadership, he has paid the price many times over, and, without power or patronage to dispense, he has retained the loyalty of freedom lovers all over the world.

Cardinal Mindszenty happens to be a Hungarian. He happens to be a Catholic. But he fought for the freedom of *all* men, regardless of faith or nation. The principles he stands for — with his mind, body and spirit — are universal and eternal. He is truly a man for all seasons.

Much has been written about Cardinal Mindszenty's public life, the famous trial, the brainwashing, the imprisonment. But previous accounts have been written from the outside looking in. This book is a firsthand report from a Hungarian who was there at his side — in the Cardinal's younger years when he was a parish priest, in his glorious days of high drama, and in intimate hours in his mother's home.

This book gives us a true picture of Mindszenty the *man*. What were the values he found valid and lasting? What was his inner strength which enabled him to overcome "the slings and arrows of outrageous fortune"? Father Joseph Vecsey was an eyewitness who kept careful notes — and I am proud to participate in presenting his strictly factual, on-the-spot report to American readers.

It was a fellow Hungarian, Sigmund Romberg, who made Americans march to the tune: "Give me some men who are stout-hearted men who will fight for the right." Cardinal Mindszenty is a stout-hearted man who has always fought for the right. The rights he fought for are the same fundamental values that made America a great nation. If we want to keep the treasure we have, let us heed his lesson of leadership.

Phyllis Schlafly

Foreword

JOSEPH CARDINAL MINDSZENTY is a Hungarian of enormous significance for all mankind.

Other great men of Hungary have been benefactors of humanity because of their achievements or their defense of personal and national values. But it is Cardinal Mindszenty who has come to symbolize the defense of universal and eternal values.

His 23 years of captivity in Budapest are a constant reminder to the Free World of the evil and danger of Communism — always ready to crush that freedom of spirit which is the basis of human dignity and, indeed, of all human culture.

His very name, Mindszenty, expresses his defense of individual liberty against tyranny. When the Nazis instituted a campaign to induce Hungarians of German descent to discard their Hungarian names and take German names instead, the man who was born Joseph Pehm expressed his defiance of the Nazis by dropping the name which revealed his German ancestry and adopting instead the Hungarian name of Joseph Mindszenty. Taken from his native village of Mindszent, this name more accurately reflects the fact that his people have been Hungarian natives for some 400 years.

The career of Cardinal Mindszenty is strongly linked with the life of a country woman of deep spirituality and sound common sense — his mother. The son inherited not only his mother's features, but also the basic traits of her character. By her sacrifices and prayers, she prepared him for his great place in history. As Cardinal Mindszenty wrote in the foreword of his book *The Mother:* "Whatever I have become is due to the merits and prayers of my mother."

It is my hope that this book will give readers a realistic insight into the everyday life of the people who live under Communist tyranny. The record of inhuman treatment and cruelty behind the Iron Curtain is often difficult for those in the Free World to believe. So that the reader will know I am an eyewitness chronicler, I have described my own relationship with Cardinal Mindszenty and with his mother, whom I affectionately called Mother Mindszenty or Mother Barbara.

Corroborative evidence of Communist oppression is presented in the Appendix by the *Diary of Sister Adelaide,* who was also a participant in the events involving Cardinal Mindszenty and his mother.

Cardinal Mindszenty's valiant struggle to save the Catholic Church in Hungary is important to everyone in the Free World, no matter what his faith. In order to understand fully the reality of Communism's war on religion, it is necessary to study this case history of how diabolical and deceitful tactics were used to transform man's natural religious inclinations into an instrument of the Communist state.

The content of this book is the drama of real history. I have simply and plainly recorded the facts as I saw them, without embellishment or theatrics. My only aim is to be a faithful historian and, in a spirit of humility and fidelity, to be a witness to the truth.

Joseph Vecsey

CHAPTER 1

The First Imprisonment

"When did you first learn about your son's arrest?" I asked.

"In 1919, a few days after it happened," Mother Mindszenty replied. "It took the pastor of Zalaegerszeg several days to find out about the events in Szombathely, and then he notified me. The revolutionaries did not dare to arrest Joseph in Zalaegerszeg where he was a religion teacher in the high school. The whole town knew my son and everybody respected and loved him, including the young people and the workers. That is why the Communists waited until they could catch him alone. They found their moment when he traveled to Szombathely on February 9, 1919 to transact some church business for his pastor.

"Having completed his mission, he planned to take the afternoon train home. Just as he boarded the train, he was seized by two plainclothes policemen who took him directly to the county office. There he was questioned by a Mr. Obal who tried to terrify my son by threatening him and asking him why he was writing and speaking against the Revolution. He meant the October Revolution of 1918. Under the flag of this Red Revolution, irresponsible extremist elements had within three months destroyed much of Hungary's wealth and productivity.

"Joseph did not answer his interrogator. Mr. Obal became more and more irritated and demanded a reply. Finally my son said only, 'Because it is my duty to spread the truth.' "

Monsignor Géfin interjected, "What was the real reason for your son's arrest?"

Mother Mindszenty continued: "The revolutionaries were very angry at him because they found it impossible to organize any successful revolutionary units. They were unable to win over the youth or the workers. The Communists believed that Joseph's pastoral work was partly responsible for this. And that

9

was true! He gave lectures, sermons and, most important, he edited a weekly newspaper. He had founded the *Zala County News* even before the Revolution. This paper was widely read and supported throughout the region. I don't need to tell you that this newspaper was an outspoken critic of destructive and extremist elements. No wonder my son was arrested!"

Monsignor Géfin questioned her further, "Can you tell us the story of how your son once dispersed a large crowd of people?"

"Oh yes," she replied. "That was another reason why the Communists were against him. When Joseph was walking home one day, he passed through the town square and saw an enormous crowd of people. The workers had been ordered by their bosses to attend this meeting to hear a speech by a Party leader from Budapest. Coming closer, my son heard the Communist speaker thundering against the 'reactionary clergy.'

"The next moment, the church bell started ringing the Angelus. The Communist speaker seemed unnerved by this. Joseph seized this moment of hesitation and in his strongest voice started to pray the Angelus. The whole crowd joined him and, by the first *Ave Maria*, everyone was praying loudly.

"At the end of the Angelus, my son made the Sign of the Cross and went home. The entire crowd did the same."

"How long was he in custody?" I asked.

"Actually, for only ten days because the youth and workers of Zalaegerszeg protested so strongly. I personally brought him the news of these protests. He was detained by two policemen in the Bishop's house which had been occupied by the revolutionaries. Being natives of Zalaegerszeg, these policemen were kind enough to let me talk to my son. I was happy to learn that he had not been broken by his captors. He told me that the Communists had hoped by arresting him to win his collaboration or, failing that, to force him out of their way.

"Their plan came to a head on the tenth day after his arrest. My son was called to the telephone on February 19 by the revolutionary chief in Zalaegerszeg who offered this proposition. Joseph would be released under two conditions: that he would change his attitude toward the Revolution, and that he would never return to Zalaegerszeg. My son refused this offer and would not give in even when he was threatened with a 15-year prison sentence. His answer didn't surprise me at all.

"Finally, the chief understood he could not intimidate my son. One policeman was then called to the telephone and given his orders, which Joseph did not hear. Putting down the receiver, the policeman said, 'Follow me, Reverend Father.'

"They went up to the second floor where the policeman ordered my son to pack his belongings. Then they left the building and started toward the town square. Joseph expected to be taken to a cell in the police station.

"But it didn't happen that way. They turned down a narrow, empty side street. The policeman suddenly stopped and said, 'Reverend Father, you may go wherever you like. You are free. But don't return to Zalaegerszeg!' Then he let my son go!"

Eager to know more, I asked, "Where did he go then?"

"To Zalaegerszeg," she replied firmly. "Later, when I asked him why he didn't come home at that time, he answered that he could take orders for a new assignment only from the Bishop.

"My son then went to the railroad station to take the next train to Zalaegerszeg. But he didn't finish the trip. Halfway there, at the town of Zalalövő, the police were waiting for him and arrested him right on the train. Once again they did not dare to take him to Zalaegerszeg. The following day he was returned under guard to the occupied Bishop's house in Szombathely."

"How long was he kept in police custody?" I asked.

"Only until March 20. That was the sad day when the civil leader of the Revolution turned over power to the Communists, a tragedy which brought about 133 days of bloody terror.

"That was the so-called 'dictatorship of the proletariat.' The first step was to intimidate the people. Hostages were taken from all parts of the country, and my son was one of them. On the night of March 20, he was taken from the Bishop's house to prison. There he was kept in complete uncertainty as to his fate, along with many other Catholic laymen and civic leaders."

At this point, Monsignor Géfin asked her to tell us the story of a well-known Monsignor from nearby Kőszeg. She willingly continued.

"Finally I obtained permission to visit my son. When I arrived at the prison, I was ordered to wait under a window near the entrance. There I first saw Monsignor Stephen Kincs, the pastor in Kőszeg, who was also a prisoner. It wasn't hard for him to guess that I was waiting to see a prisoner. He asked me whom I was waiting for. I said I was Father Mindszenty's mother and was waiting to see him. Monsignor Kincs liked to tease. Very solemnly he looked me up and down and said, 'What kind of an education did you give your son that made him end up in prison?'

"At first I didn't answer him. When he continued to tease me, I finally said, 'Monsignor's mother can't boast about *her* son, either!' He laughed heartily. I'm sure he told this story later to many people."

"How long did Father Mindszenty remain in prison?" Monsignor Géfin asked.

"Until May 19. That was the day he was escorted to Zala-egerszeg. The next day he was freed and told what was expected from him. He was ordered to work for good relationships between Church and State. He was told that, since he was a son of the common people, he must work for the 'dictatorship of the proletariat.' He was warned that his future would depend on his collaboration, and he was forbidden to meet with anyone the Communists considered 'reactionary elements.' He was expressly prohibited from seeing certain leaders such as the chief of the medical staff or various lawyers.

"My son made no answer to these warnings but left the office without a word. The next day, however, he gave his answer by openly visiting these men in their offices in broad daylight. This was his way of showing the Communists that he was not going to collaborate with them in any way whatsoever.

"Of course, Joseph was watched. Before the day was over, he received a summons. He was ordered to leave town and go home to Mindszent. From that time on, he was under house arrest.

"I was waiting for him at the station when he arrived, and naturally was glad to have him at home. He was glad that I would know where he was, but it was very hard for him to be so limited in carrying out the work assigned him by the Bishop.

"In our village, Joseph was a great help to the pastor. Although he had to report to the Village Hall twice a day, he was able to give public talks to the people. There was not one Communist in our village.

"Our village people still talk about his speeches. One of his sayings which continues to be quoted in our region is, 'Remember, if power remains in the hands of the Communists, even your scythe and spade will be stamped: *Government property!*'

"The Communist terror of this 'dictatorship of the proletariat' collapsed on August 2. But while the Communists were in power, Joseph's life was in constant danger."

I was impressed with Mother Mindszenty's well-chosen words. She had a natural simplicity without guile. She held my attention because what she said was interesting, and so was the way she said it. Her memory was remarkable. Her answers to our questions about Father Joseph Mindszenty's 1919 captivity were precise and direct. She led the conversation most of the time, often responding tactfully in place of her husband.

Our interview took place in the so-called "first room," a parlor typical of large peasant homes. Mother Mindszenty served us homemade wine and home-baked cookies, obviously delighted that we had come to see her.

Father Mindszenty's parents' home was large and well-kept, much like most of the other houses in the village of Mindszent. An attractive, wrought-iron fence and gate of carved wood enclosed the front garden, full of roses. The master of the house had awaited our arrival in the back yard, and showed us around before inviting us inside. The yard had an old-fashioned but carefully-built wall, a number of decorative trees, some fruit trees, many flowers, and a few small shelters for doves. Behind the yard was a vegetable garden, and beyond that were the farm buildings for storing corn and hay and for housing various animals.

I had just completed my first year of theological studies at Peter Pázmány University in Budapest. In that summer of 1934, Monsignor Géfin, the Vice Rector of the Szombathely Seminary, asked me to spend two weeks of my vacation with him in Mindszent, the village in western Hungary where Father Mindszenty was born.

Monsignor Géfin had written a history of our diocese of Szombathely and planned a second volume which required research on prominent diocesan priests. He knew about the influence of Father Mindszenty's mother on her son's vocation and

The house where Cardinal Mindszenty was born. Joseph Mindszenty was born March 29, 1892 in Mindszent, a village in Vas County where his ancestors had immigrated four centuries before.

wanted to interview her in order to complete his research from first-hand sources.

During meals at the local rectory where Monsignor Géfin and I were staying, conversation often turned to the village's most eminent son, Father Mindszenty, and his family. I heard there that both his parents were orphans. At the time of their marriage, his father, John Pehm, was 26 years old and his mother, nee Barbara Kovács, was 16. Combining their inherited lands, they owned 15 acres. They cultivated this land themselves from the beginning of their marriage. The work was not easy, but with hard work and prudent investment of resources, they made their land productive and eventually enlarged their acreage.

Father Mindszenty's father, in addition to taking care of his own farm and expanding it, was also active in village affairs. As a young man, he was elected the village judge. After this term was finished, he served as lay chairman of the parochial school board for more than a decade. When I first met him, he was 70 years old and still supervised the labor on the family farm and participated in the public life of the village. He was a volunteer official in the Department of Orphan Care. His son later wrote: "My father did this work enthusiastically, grateful for being able to raise his own children."[1]

Father Mindszenty's mother worked side by side with her husband in the fields, as well as doing the household tasks and teaching her six children. As Father Mindszenty expressed it later in his book *The Mother*, she was the pivot about whom the family revolved and from whom all the family drew strength and spirit.

A woman of kindly character and great patience, Mother Mindszenty was gifted most of all with an indomitable will to surmount all difficulties. On that Sunday afternoon when I first met her, it was easy to see that Father Mindszenty had inherited both her features and her character.

The church where Cardinal Mindszenty was baptized. Cardinal Mindszenty was baptized in this parish church of Mindszent. Here he made his First Confession and First Communion; here he received Confirmation and first served as an altar boy. In 1915 he said his first Mass in this church.

CHAPTER 2

The Hard-Working Pastor

In 1939, the year after I was ordained a priest, I was assigned as an assistant in the Zalaegerszeg church where Father Mindszenty was pastor. In his rectory I had spent many hours as a student, then as a seminarian. My first pastoral work was under his direction.

Pastor Mindszenty was a dynamic leader in providing services for his parishioners. He had a rare ability to win the cooperation of all the other priests for religious and social projects. It didn't take me long to realize that I was part of a well-organized and highly effective pastoral service.

Father Mindszenty made a great impression on me by his forceful personality, his ascetic way of life, his apostolic zeal, and his tremendous endurance. The tasks he entrusted to me gave me experience and practical knowledge. Whenever a moral, theological or legal problem came up, Father Mindszenty was always available to discuss the questions with us. Besides directing our parochial work, he regularly conducted conferences for priests at which he discussed the problems of the whole Catholic Church, and especially of the Church in Hungary, its policies and administration. He guided us in finding practical solutions for pressing political, social and cultural questions.

Our parish included the town of Zalaegerszeg and four neighboring villages. The majority of the 15,000 parishioners lived in the town and were office workers, manual laborers, or shopkeepers. Farmers and agricultural workers lived in the four villages.

Father Mindszenty knew almost everyone, whether or not they were Catholics. Whenever a family was in need, spiritually or financially, he was promptly notified by one of his zealous lay apostles. Either he or an assistant visited the family immediately. Father Mindszenty was particularly anxious to be called to every sickbed. He was so conscientious and alert that no one in his parish died without the Last Sacraments. The annual parish spiritual report showed his perfect record.

When I was sent to Zalaegerszeg, there were 12 priests serving the parish. Before Father Mindszenty became pastor, only five had been assigned to the town. In his first years, however, Father Mindszenty brought in four new priests to teach religion, plus a hospital chaplain. He also built a large monastery and church for the Franciscan Fathers, two of whom regularly assisted in parish work. He was thus able to provide many more Masses on Sundays and holydays, plus frequent opportunities for Confession, in the town's two large churches and several chapels.

With this larger number of priests, Father Mindszenty could provide competent priest-leaders for his spiritual and social associations. He built a spacious parish hall where these groups could meet for a growing number of activities. Here he organized various educational and recreational programs for young people after school hours. Father Mindszenty was the moderator of the League for Men and of the Congregation of Mary for women. He kept in close contact with all the other associations through conferences with their leaders and by attending their important meetings.

The indefatigable Father Mindszenty achieved real spiritual success in his parish. Not only did the women and children faithfully fulfill their religious duties, but also the laborers and office workers. Even many of the intelligentsia received the Sacraments frequently.

From his first years as pastor, Father Mindszenty had worked diligently to overcome the religious indifference of the town's liberals. He brought in well-known speakers and he organized study programs in theology. He conducted yearly retreats separately for men and for women. He invited the best orators in Hungary as retreat-masters and lecturers, including Bishop Ottokár Prohászka and Father Béla Bangha, S.J.

One day I asked a judge, who also served as lay chairman of our parish board, what was Father Mindszenty's secret in winning over so many of the intelligentsia to pursue an active spiritual life. The judge's answer revealed his own frank admiration for Father Mindszenty's energetic spiritual leadership, and particularly for his perseverance:

"At first we were puzzled and found it difficult to figure out what he wanted. We often said to each other: 'Why does this young pastor let us have no rest? Why does he pressure us with every means to get to Heaven?'"

Our rectory was a model of order and discipline. Masses, ceremonies, meetings, religion classes, and meals were all started on time. Our pastor expected much more self-discipline from the priests than from the laity.

I learned this the hard way — on May 10, 1940. I was on call that week and one of my duties was to administer the Sacrament of Baptism, if so arranged, at 2:30 every afternoon. It was the day the Germans invaded Belgium and Holland. I wanted to hear the 2:30 news on the radio. I had previously told the sacristan that I would arrive for the Baptisms after only a slight delay.

From his window, Father Mindszenty saw the godparents standing with the babies outside the sacristy after the tower clock had chimed. He suspected that the priest-on-duty was late. He confronted me in the corridor.

"Father Assistant, where are you going?"

"To baptize."

"When did you learn there were babies to be baptized?"

"At 2:25 when the sacristan came and told me."

"And why are you going only now?"

"I wanted to hear the newscast of the Nazi invasion of Belgium and Holland."

"Father, please take note. No matter what happens in the rest of the world, the time of Baptisms at our rectory remains at 2:30."

Later that afternoon, Father Mindszenty came to see me and with fatherly concern explained the importance of order and punctuality in parish services, and why it is so important for a

The Szombathely Cathedral and Seminary. Cardinal
Mindszenty took his theology training in this Seminary
and was ordained a priest in this Cathedral on June
12, 1915 by Bishop John Mikes.

The parish church of Zalaegerszeg. Cardinal Mindszenty
was pastor of this church from October 1, 1919 until
March 4, 1944. It was built by Martin Padányi Biró,
Bishop of Veszprém, in the 18th century. Zalaegerszeg ▶
was part of the Veszprém diocese until 1777 when a
separate diocese was established in Szombathely.

priest to be dependable. He himself was always careful to keep every appointment on time, regardless of whether it was with someone important or unimportant.

He was a hard worker and fortunate to have excellent health. He was never ill during the three years I was his assistant.

One severe winter night, he was called to the bedside of a sick parishioner in danger of death. A snowstorm had made it impossible to use a car or even a horse-coach. With the help of one hardy volunteer, he actually shoveled his way an amazing distance across the countryside to bring the Blessed Sacrament to the dying man.

He trained his priests to carry out their duties no matter what. We had another harsh winter in 1940. A snowstorm lasting several days halted all traffic in town. I was scheduled to conduct religion classes and a parochial school meeting in one of the villages. I was ready to leave early in the morning, but the driver did not want to risk the trip. He was especially afraid of the last part of the journey where the road was quite steep. He asked me to report this to Father Mindszenty. I went to his office and told him what the driver had said.

He listened, went to the window, and without giving any order, quietly said, "The weather is certainly bad. But it was for such circumstances that the proverb was born, 'Traveler, go ahead.'"

We started our trip in a horse-drawn coach and made it to the bottom of that treacherous hill. Then the driver couldn't find the dirt road, covered as it was with a three-day accumulation of snow. Nor could we find any path to continue on foot. We finally spotted a farm where we asked shelter for our horses. I borrowed the driver's heavy boots and proceeded to hike toward the school. When I arrived, only one teacher was there and no students at all. I waited till noon, then called on the lay chairman of the school board at his home who was astonished to see me.

I finally arrived home, several hours later than usual. As soon as Father Mindszenty saw me, he gave me hot tea and asked what had happened. After I told him the details, he said,

"Sometimes we have to prove to our parishioners that a storm does not easily discourage our priests."

As pastor of the church in the county seat, Father Mindszenty was an ex officio member of both the town and county councils. He exercised great personal influence in both organizations, and his motions were usually passed. He used his influence whenever he felt it was needed to promote justice or charity. He repeatedly attacked social injustices and Government abuses.

In 1933, for example, it was difficult to buy small lots of arable land because of the remnants of the old feudal system. A private owner, Count Festetics, had put 1,500 acres of his land up for sale. The small farmers in the county organized a cooperative to buy this land for individual families. However, all 1,500 acres were sold to a wealthy member of Parliament. Father Mindszenty made a motion in the county council to nullify the sale. Although his motion passed, the case went to the national Government where the rich politician was upheld. Father Mindszenty then wrote an open letter in the press criticizing this unjust decision. He was not able to reverse it, but his energetic intervention on behalf of the small landowners was appreciated by the people.

Father Mindszenty was responsible for all organized charity in the county. He built a home for the aged poor. People wanted to name this home after him, but he declined. Nothing was further from his desires than to promote a personality cult.

Every year he helped about 35 students finance their high school studies. He organized collections for this and donated from his own resources. He generously supported many social and cultural projects. He opened a printing shop in the parish for his weekly newspaper which he planned to transform into a daily.

To make sure his newspaper would be independent, he refused to accept any financial aid from the Government.

After completing the parish hall, the home for the elderly, and the Franciscan Monastery, he built a large convent and school for the teaching Sisters of Notre Dame. After all this was completed, he enlarged and modernized his own rectory, adding a third floor to provide quarters for the five priests who taught religion in the town. He reorganized the parish's financial resources. When some parish lands were sold for urban development, he used the receipts to buy another farm of 120 acres in Ságod for the benefit of the parish.

The Franciscan Church and Monastery in Zalaegerszeg. Cardinal Mindszenty's first important accomplishment as a parish priest was to build this Church and Monastery. Later he formed a new parish from his own large one and placed it in the hands of these Franciscan Fathers.

Several times each year, Father Mindszenty's parents were guests in his rectory. In addition, his mother came more frequently to spend a week or so in Zalaegerszeg. In the spring of 1940, I escorted her on a visit to the new farm in Ságod. She was eager to see its progress since the farm had previously been quite neglected.

As I went to Ságod once a week to teach religion, I could assure her that the farm was developing rapidly. A long building had been built containing a three-room apartment for each laborer's family. Then the barns, stables, silos, and other storage buildings were added. Father Mindszenty had personally discussed all the plans with the contractors. He insisted on including the most modern sanitary and safety techniques.

Mother Mindszenty asked me if the workers were industrious and dependable, and I assured her they were, and in addition were quite satisfied with their homes and wages. Their living and working conditions were superior to those of the other agricultural workers in the area. Father Mindszenty hired more men than the usual minimum in order to protect them from being overworked, and those with numerous children were especially welcome.

When we arrived at the farm, Mother Mindszenty was surprised at the change in such a short time. She first visited some of the families of the workers. She would chat with the mother and give candy and chocolate to the children. The women told her of their contentment and gratitude to Father Mindszenty. When she finished her tour of the apartments, she complimented "the good and hard-working people who keep their homes clean."

She wanted to see the animals, so I took her to the stables. She carefully inspected the cows, the hogs, and the chicken coops. She was well satisfied and noted that "the big machines are expensive, but they do a better job of cultivating the land and they make the lives of the workers easier." We took a horse-drawn coach to see the fields. I was surprised at how knowledgeable she was in discussing the probable yields of wheat, hay, potatoes, turnips and other vegetables.

As we rode home, she looked back at the fields and said: "My son has a beautiful and valuable farm. He needs it to cover all his big expenses — the newspaper, the buildings, all those students, and the new home for the aged. The superintendent told me how the people wanted to name it after my son, but he would not let them do it. I like to come to Zalaegerszeg and see the fruits of my son's work.

"There was a time when I used to think — and so did my two daughters — why couldn't Joseph help on our own family farm? Both my daughters have had to work so hard, and we could have used his help.

"But I know this is better. My son is happier this way. And I am, too. Anyway, the truth is that he has always been there with a helping hand whenever his sisters really needed it."

Notre Dame Convent and School in Zalaegerszeg. Pastor Mindszenty invited the teaching Sisters of Notre Dame to open this school with his financial help. It had an enrollment of 1,000 pupils. In 1948 the Communists expropriated it along with 3,100 other Catholic schools in Hungary. Two years later, the Sisters were arrested in a night raid on the Convent and sent to concentration camps together with some 2,000 other priests and nuns.

CHAPTER 3

Father Mindszenty the Author

Besides his many pastoral and social activities, Father Mindszenty found time to do quite a bit of writing. In addition to his frequent articles in diocesan and secular papers, he completed two books. One was a 500-page biography of an 18th century Bishop of Veszprém, Martin Biró, which was rich in historical detail. His other book was entitled *The Mother* and went through three different editions.

Even as a young man, Father Mindszenty displayed a special love for his mother. In 1909 he had been given a class assignment on the literary theme "The Joys and Sorrows of a Mother." He wrote an essay of six pages which drew this comment from his teacher: "Your sentiments are genuine. Your essay is well written. Excellent."

In 1915 he expanded his early essay to 100 pages and entered it in a contest sponsored by his Seminary's St. Augustine Literary Club. He won first prize, with a suggestion from the jury that the manuscript be published.

The following year, after he was ordained a priest and assigned to a parish in the village of Paty, Father Mindszenty rewrote the entire article and published it. It was an immediate sellout; a second printing was ordered the same year.

The following years were not conducive to literary achievement. On January 26, 1917, his Bishop assigned him to Zalaegerszeg as a high school religion teacher. His job also required classes for students after school hours which used up the rest of his time. War, revolution, arrest, and imprisonment, all deprived him of the time and quiet needed for writing. Immediately after the collapse of the Revolution in 1919, he became the pastor in Zalaegerszeg. He was then 27 years old, a young man faced with the tremendous task of ministering to his flock in a large parish where up-to-date leadership had been lacking for several years.

The new pastor was eager to raise the spiritual level of his people and he dedicated himself to his work. This included the editing of the diocesan newspaper, the *Zala County News*. He always personally wrote the column on spiritual matters.

Father Mindszenty's busy schedule was somewhat eased once he built the Franciscan Monastery and increased the number of priests serving the town. Just about that time, however, the Historical Society (Monsignor Géfin was one of its active members) asked Father Mindszenty to write a biography of a former Bishop of Veszprém, Bishop Martin Biró. A busy pastor could do this only by squeezing extra moments out of a crowded schedule. He used his vacations for research in libraries and archives. The large amount of material he accumulated had to be worked on in the late night hours after his daily parochial work was done.

In spite of a shortage of time, Father Mindszenty examined every available primary and secondary source. After five years of painstaking work, his 500-page book was published in 1934.

The book is described as follows in *Documentation Concerning Cardinal Mindszenty:* "This book of half-a-thousand pages is an excellent example of a scholarly historical monograph written with a meticulous understanding of the social conditions in western Hungary in the 18th century. It is the most important key to Cardinal Mindszenty as a historian."[1]

Professor Thomas Bogyay, a leading contemporary Hungarian historian, commented: "The above description is short and accurate. This book by Mindszenty is the definitive work on its subject. The *Bibliography of Hungarian History*, edited in Hungary in 1954, could not ignore this work."[2]

Professor Bogyay went on to describe Cardinal Mindszenty's skill as a historian: "Essential to a historian are the ability to synthesize his research and the power of creative description. These qualities make the difference between the historian and the dilettante. The first quality derives from a deep desire to learn about the past; the scholar is never satisfied with superficial events, but strives to provide a living picture of the past — not as a fiction writer would write it, but as an objective researcher interested in the truth. The power of creative description is a quality possessed by an authentic artist who desires to re-create the past. A fine example of a writer possessing both qualities is the author of the Bíró biography."

Professor Bogyay went on to state in his review: "The hero of the book is characterized in the introduction as a man of will power. This judgment is reinforced by the author's conscientious use of a plethora of research which he has subjected to careful critical analysis. Five pages of his extensive bibliography are devoted to a listing of primary sources, many of which are the result of the author's original investigation.

"Before Mindszenty, no other historian had the courage to evaluate the complex personality and career of Bishop Martin Padányi Bíró. That was one reason why Mindszenty insisted on using first-hand sources to corroborate his findings. He used the documents of 45 archives for his biography, including those of the Vatican, the State Archives of Vienna, the National Archives of Budapest, the local archives of various counties, Catholic rectories, Calvinist parishes, monastic libraries, and other collections. . . .

"Mindszenty always displays that essential element of a true historian, namely, *insight:* the understanding that people of earlier times were different, that social conditions were different, and so were the possibilities for carrying out God's plan. This is why he carefully measured the controversial deeds of the Bishop (and his opponents) against the background of the ideas and customs of the 18th century. It is not any accident that the author of the Bíró monograph used the present tense frequently. He wanted to bring the historical past as close as possible to the reader and involve the reader as a participant in the climactic events unfolding before him. . . .

"With keen observation, the author describes incidents and problems perennial to the Church and human society. However, he carefully avoids sensationalism or oversimplification in his treatment of complex human motivation. In the way he handles historical material, Mindszenty proves himself a historical artist."[3]

Joseph Mindszenty as titular Abbot of Porno. This title was given for his excellent service to the church in 1924 by his Bishop, John Mikes.

◄ **The parish church in Ják.** This beautiful Romanesque church dates from the 12th century and stimulated Cardinal Mindszenty's studies in history and art.

After his book *The Life and Times of Martin Biró, Bishop of Veszprém* was published, Pastor Mindszenty devoted his spare hours to preparing a third edition of his book *The Mother*. His original plan was to expand and publish the work in three volumes. He published the first volume of the third edition early in 1941 and the second volume at Christmastime in 1942. World War II, his consecration as Bishop, and later elevation as Cardinal-Primate, prevented him from completing the third volume.

On March 19, 1941, the feast day of his Patron Saint, Joseph Mindszenty gave a beautifully-bound copy of the first volume to his mother. At a gala dinner that evening, he made a little speech taken from the introduction of the book. "I shall quote the poet," he began. " 'Throughout my life, a God-sent faithful angel has guarded my fate with endless care — my mother, the dearest mother of all.' "

"I have felt the warmth of motherly love," he continued. "God gave me a good mother who took care of me by hard work and reared me with prayerful spirit; she prayed for me always, and shed many tears for my vocation. Both in and outside the home, I learned how holy are the wrinkles of love on the face of a mother.

"Since I do not know if I can ever repay my debt to her, I have sought to give her this token of my gratitude. With St. Augustine I repeat: 'I became Your servant, O Lord, because I was the son of Your servant. Whatever I have become is due to the merits and prayers of my mother.' "

His mother accepted the book with happy tears in her eyes. She embraced him and responded: "Thank you, Joseph, for this beautiful book. May God reward you. I know your book will help many mothers to find counsel, consolation and strength in time of suffering. I know how much of your precious time you spent in writing this much-needed book. We have seen so little of you in the last several years. Thank God you have finished it and now, hopefully, perhaps you can come more frequently to see your old parents."

While Mother Mindszenty was at the rectory, we had many discussions. I talked with her about the new book, hoping to learn more details about her son's life. I had helped to proof-read *The Mother*, so I knew it well. It was easy for me to find the parts obviously written about her.

When I read her the introduction, her reaction was typical. She said that the sentiments about her were beautiful, but she was most pleased with the way her son gave credit to God. "God is the One who gives mother and child to each other and enables us to live in mutual love."

Then I read her these lines from the book: "When a small boy gets adventurous near a pond and, like a frog, jumps into the water, but gets caught in some machinery left there by a local industry and cries for help, who comes to rescue him but his mother, wading right into the pond to set him free?"[4]

Mother Mindszenty explained, "Yes, that actually happened. Joseph writes about it as if it were a funny story, but I can tell you it was certainly not funny at the time. I had to call the blacksmith to cut him out of the trap! My son was a lively boy who brought sunshine into all our lives."

I continued reading from Father Mindszenty's book: "Mothers are always learning and teaching. My mother taught me to serve at the altar. She was my tutor when I studied the long history of Christ's Passion. She helped me win my first prize — a coin — from my old pastor. A mother will even go so far as to learn the writing style of her child and, when he falls asleep, she will complete his homework."[5]

Mother Mindszenty interrupted to tell me that she had helped her son with his homework only in the earliest school years. Her son liked school and his teachers were always pleased with him. She recalled how proud she was to watch him serve Mass for the first time.

I then began reading passages which included Father Mindszenty's recollections as a high school student. I noticed that most of his remembrances were connected with his mother and he said very little about his father. I bluntly asked her why.

"Perhaps because his father had opposed his plans for higher education. He didn't like the idea, mainly because of the expense involved. We needed the money for the family farm. He also wanted his only son to work on the farm and help the family — to be his father's pride and joy.

"I was the one who insisted on making plans for Joseph's high school studies. When other women in the village learned about this, they gossiped about me and made cruel remarks about my excessive ambition. In the end, I won out with the help of one of my son's teachers, Mr. Fehér. He called on us one evening and told my husband it would be a great mistake not to send my son to high school. The teacher said he thought that Joseph would some day become a great Hungarian leader! After this visit, my husband relented and agreed to pay for Joseph's schooling."

I mentioned that the following passage probably alluded to the father's reluctance to let his son go to high school: "Today it is not so remarkable for a village boy to go to high school. But it was quite different 40 years ago. Most people had little sympathy for the non-conformist family which dared to send a boy on for higher education. It was a rare village where this was ever tried. People might give some superficial respect to such a family, but behind their backs they always questioned such daring."[6]

Mother Mindszenty commented, "Joseph remembers the difficulties of those first years very well, indeed."

"Do you remember," I asked, "what was the nature of your 'anxiety' which Father Mindszenty mentions in the book?"

"That was the first time I sent him off to boarding school in the big city. I still remember the day he left. The swallows were flying south. Naturally, I wanted him to go — it was what I had planned for and prayed for. And yet it was an anxious and difficult day for me when I sent my only son away to school — rather like the day a bride leaves her family home to enter an uncertain future. But, of course, a mother loves her child's welfare more than her own pleasure.

"I am quite sure that Joseph already knew at that time what a mother's love means. Otherwise, he would never have been able to describe in such a beautiful way, 40 years later, the anxiety I felt when I bade him goodbye."

"But we can read in his book," I added, "that he 'remained in my mother's care even in the distant town of Szombathely.

Every three months my mother came to visit. She always brought a real feast. In addition to her cheerful presence, she brought delicious homemade food. The cook at a royal palace could not produce any better meals.

" 'She also brought the news of a happy world now closed to me. She brought the affection of Father and my sisters, and most of all, her own love. She brought the greetings of the old priest and of my favorite teacher, and the news of people in the village and who had died.

" 'Yes, the welfare of her distant child is a mother's greatest concern and worry. Nothing gives as much good advice as a mother's goodbye kiss, and few books contain as much wise instruction as a mother's letter.' "[7]

Mother Mindszenty interrupted to say, "It really was a trying experience for me to have a son away at school. It would have been a great sorrow if he had failed in his studies. Therefore, I visited him regularly from the start. I wanted to keep posted on his progress. It was not easy for a village boy, thrown among lads from well-to-do city families and under strict professors, to rank with the best students. Thank God, Joseph received high grades from the very beginning."

Then I brought up the references in Father Mindszenty's book to the mothers of boys who choose the priesthood for their vocation: "These heroic mothers were ready to visit all the churches in the town to pray for their sons' future. They had tears in their eyes when they saw the seminarians in their white surplices. ... Then came the fateful hour of final decision about the future, a decision which vitally concerned their happiness on earth and in Heaven.

"If there is a vocation to the priesthood, wise mothers do not oppose it; they do not try to persuade their sons one way or the other. They pray and they offer their advice. They are prepared to accept their son's vocation. ... Such a mother repeats the words of the Countess Castiglione to her son who became St. Aloysius: 'Go wherever God calls you.' "[8]

"It was not an easy decision," Mother Mindszenty explained, "at the beginning of this century, in a liberal intellectual atmosphere, for a gifted boy to make a decision for the priesthood. Joseph was an avid reader and had carefully observed

Catholic spiritual and cultural trends. He was interested in religious literature, and he admired the courageous editors and scholars who wrote for Catholic newspapers. He was an active apostle for the Catholic press during his student years.

"Perhaps this was the reason why, before his high school graduation, he had wanted to become a writer in order to serve the sacred cause of the Catholic faith by his pen. When he mentioned this to me, I simply said to him, 'You know, Joseph, you can become a good author if you will first become a priest.'

"Really, I had been praying for that decision for many years. I was very happy when, after graduation, he applied and was admitted to the Seminary in Szombathely."

Golden Wedding Anniversary of the Cardinal's Parents. Cardinal Mindszenty's parents, John Pehm and Barbara Kovács, were married in January 1891. This family photograph was taken at their Golden Jubilee celebration. Cardinal Mindszenty is seated at his father's left, and his two sisters are seated at his mother's right.

Finally, I asked whether her Golden Wedding Anniversary celebration had been held in Mindszent. The book had a reference to this. "Yes," she replied, "we had our Golden Jubilee in our village last January. Everything happened just as Joseph described it in his book. He said Mass and gave us his blessing."

Then I read her this quotation: "The grandchildren are proud of their grandfather who was lay chairman of the parish board for 45 years. Although now 75 years old, he still helps care for village orphans in gratitude that his own children were not orphaned.

"Their grandmother is a fine, quiet, intelligent woman who lives always in the presence of God. For three generations, she has been, if not the head, then the heart of the family, the very axis about which the entire life of the family revolves."

Mother Mindszenty smiled and with a twinkle in her eye concluded our visit with these words: "Whatever Joseph wrote about his father is all quite true. As for me, he should have written, 'It was pleasant to see the other old one tending to her duties about the house.'"

Cardinal Mindszenty's Mother about the year 1930.

CHAPTER 4

Imprisonment by the Nazis

In the midst of World War II, on November 1, 1942, Bishop Joseph Grősz transferred me from Zalaegerszeg to Szombathely, the episcopal seat. He assigned me as Prefect in the diocesan Seminary, and also to teach religion in the public high school.

My new home was only a three-hour train trip from Zala-egerszeg, so I returned frequently. Sometimes I visited my relatives there. More often, I brought information and materials for Father Mindszenty's newspaper which had become the Catholic paper for the whole diocese.

Now a Monsignor, he strove diligently to preserve the independence of his paper, and he succeeded until the very end. His was one of the very few newspapers which carried articles critical of both Communism and Nazism, exposing their dangerous ideas and social programs. The editorial staff of the newspaper was headed by Monsignor Francis Rogács, later the Bishop of Pécs in southern Hungary. I became a sort of informal messenger to and from Zalaegerszeg and developed a warm friendship with the editorial staff. On most visits, I was able to have a good talk with the chief editor, Monsignor Mindszenty. If our conversation lasted long enough, he always invited me to stay for supper and overnight.

During this period, I saw his parents frequently. Being a dutiful son, Monsignor Mindszenty had arranged for medical care for his elderly parents. His parents enjoyed the hospitality of the rectory when they had a doctor's appointment in town. They were also there on important holydays such as Christmas, on the feast of St. Joseph (Monsignor's patron saint), as well as at harvest time. When special guests arrived, the parents were always graciously included at the dinner table.

I vividly recall the grape harvest of 1943. It was the custom in western Hungary to hold a family reunion after the grapes had been picked and the wine-making started. Monsignor

Mindszenty had a one-acre vineyard, and he participated in this local custom by inviting his former Seminary companions for an annual dinner. He included other friends who were county and town officials, in addition to a few other priests. His mother was the hostess for these yearly dinner parties at the Zalaegerszeg rectory.

Monsignor Mindszenty's former schoolmates were well aware of his abilities and admired his exemplary priestly life and apostolic activities. In high spirits at the October 1943 dinner, various guests spoke up about his energy, talents and experience, and suggested that perhaps the time had come for a further promotion. For several months, three Hungarian dioceses had been without a bishop: Veszprém, Szombathely, and Szeged. Monsignor Mindszenty made no comment, but that didn't stop his friends from talking. I learned later from other sources that he had been nominated by the Papal Nuncio for either of two dioceses.

There had been a long delay in the appointment of these three bishops. It became known that the possible nomination of Monsignor Mindszenty had caused the postponement. It is now clear that the Regent of the Hungarian Government, Admiral Nicholas Horthy, had used his veto. The Hungarian head of state had enjoyed this power ever since Pope Pius XI had granted it after the episcopal appointment of Cardinal Serédi.

Admiral Horthy opposed Monsignor Mindszenty's appointment as Bishop because the latter often spoke and wrote against the Government's inadequate political and social programs. During the 25 years Father Mindszenty was pastor in Zalaegerszeg, the members of Parliament elected from that town had always been members of the Christian Party. He always supported them, as well as every movement among the people in behalf of social justice. He enthusiastically assisted such organizations as the KALOT (Catholic Farmers Association), the EMSZO (Catholic Workers Movement), and the KIOE (Young Christian Workers).

The Primate, Cardinal Serédi, did not favor Monsignor Mindszenty because of a certain memorandum written by a national assembly of priests which urged the Church in Hungary to show more initiative and become more active in social and cultural problems. Monsignors Mindszenty and Szentkirályi had been selected by the assembly to present the memorandum to Cardinal Serédi. The Cardinal, an introvert, became rather sensitive about the memorandum's criticism of his lack of action on social issues.

As might be expected, the Horthy Government pushed its own nominees for appointment as bishops. The Hungarian Bishops' Conference also had the right of nomination, but this body was more or less controlled by Cardinal Serédi. The Papal Nuncio, Archbishop Angelo Rotta, knew exactly what was going on, and did everything he could to secure the promotion of Monsignor Mindszenty. The Papal Nuncio was helped in this effort by the retired former Ordinary of Szombathely, Bishop John Mikes. Characteristically, Monsignor Mindszenty made absolutely no move in his own behalf.

Due to the Papal Nuncio's vigilance and Bishop Mikes' support, Admiral Horthy finally realized that Monsignor Mindszenty could not be bypassed and agreed to a compromise. If Monsignor Alexander Kovács were appointed to the See of Szombathely, Admiral Horthy would then agree to Monsignor Mindszenty's episcopal appointment.

This was the background behind the appointment of the three bishops on March 4, 1944. Monsignor Mindszenty became Bishop of Veszprém in western Hungary, Monsignor Kovács became Bishop of Szombathely on the western border, and Father Andrew Hamvas (Cardinal Serédi's nominee) became Bishop of Csanád on the southern border.

The following day, after Monsignor Géfin, now Rector of
the Major Seminary, phoned Bishop-elect Mindszenty to con-
gratulate him, he called me to the telephone, too. The Bishop-
elect asked me to come to Zalaegerszeg to help him pack his
manuscripts and library.

When I arrived, I found his mother hard at work. She had
just prepared a complete inventory of all the furniture and
equipment in the rectory. Seeing me, she stopped for a little
rest. She told me her son had wired her immediately upon being
notified of his appointment, and had asked her to come and
help. She had come promptly, knowing how much work there
would be in such a large house.

I congratulated her on her son's promotion. First she showed
her happiness, but then became very serious. She pointed out
what a difficult situation he was in. She sadly told me she
was certain that her son could not escape imprisonment,
whether Hungary fell under Nazi control or to the Communists. Although I knew she was right, I tried to cheer her.

It didn't take long to pack the new Bishop's personal belongings. Then we packed his manuscripts, including much material
for the prospective third volume of his book *The Mother*. He
left a large part of his books and furniture, and everything
at the farm in Ságod including the animals and machines, to
the pastor who succeeded him.

Then there were his immense correspondence and the files
concerning the anti-Nazi resistance movement, as well as numerous folders containing his sermons and speeches. In packing
Bishop Mindszenty's files, I learned a great deal about how he
did his intellectual work. From his first years as a priest, he
prepared each sermon or speech in writing with the greatest
care, although he never used any written notes in giving his
speeches (except later when he was Primate of Hungary and
had to give long academic discourses). In most cases he wrote
a very detailed outline, and quite frequently he wrote out his
sermons and speeches word for word.

At that time, it was nearly the third anniversary of the
occupation of Yugoslavia by Hitler. Several of his army units
were noisily passing through Zalaegerszeg, and the Nazi occupation of Hungary was imminent.

After the following Sunday's High Mass, Bishop Mindszenty phoned to tell me he had just received information that both of us had been put on the Nazi blacklist. He had been singled out because he was a leader in the ideological movement headed by Count Paul Teleki urging resistance to the Nazis in western Hungary. I was marked because I worked with him in the same project.

After a short discussion, Bishop Mindszenty said that I could flee the country but, as a pastor, he was obliged to remain. A few days later, we heard that the Nazis were so well satisfied with their success in inducing their puppet government to bring Hungary into the war that they planned to leave the black-listed priests alone.

Ten days after Bishop Mindszenty's appointment, he turned over his parish to an administrator and went to Veszprém to study the conditions and problems of a great diocese which had been without a Bishop for nine months. The Nazi occupation was so imminent that he asked the Primate, Cardinal Serédi, to consecrate the three new bishops as soon as possible.

Joseph Mindszenty's consecration as Bishop took place on March 25, 1944 in the Basilica of Esztergom in northern Hungary. Naturally, the new Bishop's proud mother was present. She had spent much time studying the ritual for the ceremony. Later she described it for the rest of her family and her fellow villagers with remarkable detail and accuracy.

I had two opportunities to visit with Bishop Mindszenty in his new episcopal residence in Veszprém. Soon after his installation, he called me to come and tell him about certain events in the Szombathely diocese which had worried him. I arrived at suppertime, as he had told me the only time he had free was in the evening. Right after dinner, he invited me into his library.

After we had finished our business and I had told him how pleased were the people of his former diocese about his promotion, he opened a drawer and took out some 20 letters. He had selected these because they were written by his best friends or contained the most meaningful messages. He read some of them to me and summarized the others. After the letters from bishops, heads of religious communities, old friends, professors, and well-known community leaders, he read his mother's letter last.

After more than a quarter of a century, I am still moved at recalling this letter — so simple, lucid, and rich in meaning. First, she reminded her Bishop-son of the obstacles that had to be overcome by the family in order to give him a higher education. She recalled how Mr. Fehér had persuaded the Bishop's father to undertake the expense for these studies. She recalled the decisive moment when the teacher had said, "Joseph will some day become a great Hungarian leader."

The next part of the letter contained a beautiful thanksgiving to God for her son's success in overcoming all difficulties, for his being freed from Communist captivity in 1919, and for the blessings that had been showered upon his pastoral work in Zalaegerszeg.

At the end of the letter, Mother Mindszenty again cited her son's imprisonment by the Communists, warning him that he would probably have to face even greater sufferings in the future. She concluded by saying that, if this happened while he was carrying out his great mission as Bishop, he should always be guided and strengthened by Jesus' words, "Blessed are those who suffer persecution for justice' sake."

The installation of the new Bishop of Veszprém occurred during one of the darkest days in Hungary's history. Hitler's army had occupied Hungary about a week earlier, on March 19, 1944, and forced the country to enter the war. In retaliation, the Allies began to bomb cities and industrial centers hitherto spared.

Thus it happened that the first pastoral visits of Bishop Mindszenty were accompanied by heavy bombing attacks on various targets in his diocese. In spite of the danger, he visited every parish to learn his people's problems at first hand and discuss their solutions.

At the same time, many prompt decisions had to be made about the parishes, the schools, and other church institutions. His problems were further complicated by the fact that, due to deaths or transfers, his new diocese had had four bishops within six years.

Bishop Mindszenty devoted much time to his priests. He organized retreats, days of recollection, and pastoral study programs. He was always ready to take long trips to administer the Sacrament of Confirmation. On these visits to the farthest parts of his diocese, he personally examined the management of the rectories and the quality of the pastoral work. He advised his priests to take care of the needy by establishing special charitable organizations.

He urged the adoption of a system of volunteer lay apostles who would regularly visit each family. He demanded that the churches be clean and well kept, that priests prepare good sermons and perform the liturgy well. He emphasized the necessity of his priests always being present when a parishioner was on his sickbed nearing death.

A summer of horrors began when, on Hitler's orders, the Hungarian puppet Government started the deportation of the Jews. The entire Hungarian Catholic episcopate protested this atrocity. The most vigorous and vocal protesters were Bishop Mindszenty of Veszprém and Bishop Apor of Győr. Their protests were supported by nearly 100 per cent of the Catholic priests in Hungary. This is confirmed by the following statement made by the chief of the Nazi Department of Jewish Affairs: "Reluctantly I must say that the most vigorous defenders of the Jews are the priests and ministers of all the Christian denominations. Their protests are quite numerous. The priests say they are helping the Jews because of fraternal charity."[1]

Bishop Mindszenty turned every religious house under his jurisdiction into a sanctuary for Jews hiding from the Gestapo. Even though the Nazis threatened death as punishment for those concealing Jews, Bishop Mindszenty ordered every Catholic monastery, convent, seminary, rectory, cloister, and church to open its doors to the Jews and hide them from the Gestapo. He told his fellow Catholics: "If today we do not keep sacred and inviolable the Jew's personal freedom, his common and civil rights, tomorrow we may find that we have lost our own." He called anti-Semitism "the basest tool of Nazi propaganda — a tool which seeks to undermine the very foundations of Christian civilization."[2]

In defending the Jews against the Nazis at the risk of his own life, Bishop Mindszenty was merely remaining faithful to his lifetime belief in the freedom of the individual, regardless of race or religion. Many incidents throughout his life had demonstrated his respect for the honest faith of a religious Jew, and his scorn for the man who was not faithful to his religion, whether Catholic, Protestant or Jewish.

By the fall of 1944, two-thirds of Hungary was a battlefield. The Regent of Hungary, Admiral Horthy, made a secret attempt to get Hungary out of the war by making a separate peace. When Hitler learned about this, he ordered a coup d'etat in Hungary and took Horthy into custody. Under Hitler's orders, a National Socialist Government was formed on October 15, 1944. It was a puppet Government, pathetically obeying the orders of the Nazi masters and led about like a blindfolded prisoner.

In the meantime, the Red Army was rapidly advancing toward Budapest, robbing, raping, and murdering civilians. Tens of thousands of people were frantically trying to escape from Communism by fleeing to the West. In this horrible situation, the Nazi puppet Government gave the order, "Either we destroy or we shall be destroyed."

The dreaded Nazi Gestapo began to hunt for hostages.

Upon learning that my name was again on the list, I went to Veszprém to see my brother, who was my closest relative, to discuss with him what I should do. He was an enlisted man serving at an anti-aircraft station. To my surprise, I could not locate him anywhere at the air base. Terribly upset and suspecting what might have happened to him, I hurried to see Bishop Mindszenty who had known my brother. We both feared that my brother had been arrested by the Nazis.

Fortunately, the Bishop's chancellor was on friendly terms with my brother's commanding officer and was able to find out what happened. It turned out that my brother had been detained on a very minor charge, the details of which were unclear. At any rate, the commanding officer arranged that the case be cleared from the court docket, and my brother was not only freed but given a two-week furlough.

Bishop Mindszenty was most kind to us. He invited me for supper and even found a place for me to stay overnight in the crowded city. My bed was a straw sack in the corridor of a rectory. The Bishop's own residence was crowded with refugees who had lost their homes from the bombing or had been expelled from their homes by the Nazi Army. The Bishop occupied only one room in the episcopal residence in order to make every other room available to the refugees.

When I was alone with him, he told me he planned to go to Budapest the next day where the Upper House of Parliament was convening to discuss a joint memorandum of the Bishops of Hungary. This memorandum had been signed by all the bishops in areas not yet under Communist control, and it urged the Government to end its participation in an unreasonable war.[3]

Suddenly I felt terribly worried. Excitedly I blurted out that no constructive result could be gained from angering the Nazis by such a step. Then I calmed down and begged Bishop Mindszenty not to endanger himself by such a move. I insisted that his life was too valuable, and that his leadership would be needed by the people and by the Catholic Church far more *after* the war when we would all have to live with the unpredictable, terrifying consequences.

Bishop Mindszenty's answer was simple: "The Bishops of Hungary are expected to sacrifice their lives not only for the Church, but also for their country if circumstances require it."

The following day he took the train to Budapest. I went with him to the station, and I had a sinking feeling that this was perhaps my last meeting with Bishop Mindszenty.

The political confusion in Budapest was such that it was impossible to convene the Parliament's Upper House. So, Bishop Mindszenty personally presented the memorandum to the Nazi Government.

His fate was determined by this courageous act. The Nazis immediately planned his arrest, terming him "a dangerous enemy of the Government."

On the morning of November 27, 1944, when the Bishop was in residence at his home, two officers from the county headquarters arrived to search the house and take over several rooms for Government use. Like actors in a farce, they moved with such noise and vulgarity that everyone was outraged. Their search ended with the arrest of one of the Chancery priests. The Bishop immediately protested this arrest of one of his secretaries.

A short time later, the county police chief arrived to arrest the Bishop himself. Bishop Mindszenty went immediately to his room, then solemnly appeared in his prelate's cape and biretta to receive the police.

All the priests and religious who were crowded into the Bishop's residence moved quickly to accompany their Bishop. They made it impossible for the police to hustle him into the police car. He then said he would walk to prison. So, followed by a great number of his priests, religious and seminarians, and guarded by the Nazi police, Bishop Mindszenty walked through the streets giving his blessing to the people who crowded about him. On both sides of the road, men tipped their hats and women knelt down to receive the blessing of their Bishop who was being led away by the police. Not only Catholics, but people of all religions, joined him as he walked. They were all orderly, following the Bishop as though they were in a large procession. When they reached the prison, Bishop Mindszenty turned toward the people, once again gave his blessing, and told them to return to their homes.

The next day, all 26 priests and seminarians who had followed the Bishop to prison were arrested and thrown into jail with the common criminals. Since they were all together and under the guidance of their Bishop, they continued their daily prayers and participated in the Bishop's celebration of Mass, receiving Communion from his hands. Several theology professors were in the group, so the Bishop told them to hold their classes in the prison.

In a public speech years later, Cardinal Mindszenty described how he had given the Sacrament of Holy Orders inside this Nazi prison: "The last time I ordained priests was in the basement of the Veszprém prison, which looked like a dark catacomb. What a strange ceremony! The consecrator was a prisoner; those ordained were also prisoners. The ten new priests all together had only one candle, one cassock, and one surplice — but each had a separate armed guard standing over him with a loaded gun!

"At this unusual ordination there were a few guests — all prisoners: a judge who was a devout Catholic, 16 more priests, and about 20 to 25 laymen. The date of this ordination, December 7, 1944, was the feast day of a great defender of the freedom of the Church, St. Ambrose. When I began the ceremony, I was prepared to be stopped by an air raid, or by the approaching Soviet Army, or by a sudden decision of the prison officials to take us to another prison, a possibility we had been warned of in advance. God willed that none of these occurred. All three happened later."[4]

In the meantime, under orders from my own Bishop, I was serving as an assistant in a very small village. Because I was so far out in the country, I escaped at least one planned arrest.

In the middle of winter, civilian transportation was practically non-existent. Toward the end of January 1945, one day a friend with an army car secretly gave me a ride to Szombathely. I persuaded him to make a stop on the way in Mindszent so I could see Bishop Mindszenty's mother and learn some news of her son. She was happy to see me, and I was glad to find out that she did not seem to be as worried as I had expected.

She told me the reason she seemed so calm was that she had not been left in the dark about her son's fate. She received accurate and dependable news about him almost every week. Visitor's privileges were frequently extended to the pastor of Sopron, Father Coloman Papp (later the Bishop of Győr). Father Papp would report the latest news from the prison to the retired Bishop Mikes, and from him the news eventually reached Mother Mindszenty. Just to have regular information was reassuring.

Mother Mindszenty knew that her son and all his priests had been transferred on Christmas eve to the prison of Sopronkőhida. Cardinal Mindszenty later described what happened: "Upon our arrival at the new prison on Christmas eve, my 26 priests and I were not fed for 48 hours. The wives and daughters of the police guards first wept over us; then they started to share their meager food with us. They finally brought so much food that our guards ate supper with us. They needed it, since their bags contained bullets intended for us instead of food."[5]

Mother Mindszenty had learned a great deal about the prison conditions. All the captive priests had been put into one big hall, but a small private room had been set aside for her son. He objected to being singled out and was then permitted to stay with his priests and sleep on straw on the ground, just like everybody else. He shared their prison conditions completely. He waited in line for his food as they did. He shared his spoon and cup with his fellow priests.

Meanwhile, Bishop Mindszenty saw to it that the theology classes were continued in prison. The seminarians finished their semester studies in January and passed their examinations.

Sharing with me all the news she had about her son's imprisonment, Mother Mindszenty told me she entrusted her son and his fellow prisoners to the Sacred Heart of Jesus and offered all her Masses and Rosaries for their welfare. She had great faith that the Sacred Heart would sustain them.

Who could doubt that the prayers, sacrifices and good works of a mother of such deep faith were partly responsible for her son's release! After four and a half months of captivity, on the last day of March 1945, he was freed.

Bishop Mindszenty's release from the Nazi prison occurred at the very time the Soviet Army reached the Hungarian border, thus fulfilling his dire warnings about the inevitable fate awaiting western Hungary.

Cities, villages, churches, schools, rectories, factories, and homes by the hundreds of thousands were in ruins. People everywhere were starving. No trains were running. Most of the roads were impassable and transportation was at a standstill. In addition to all this, the drunken soldiers of the Red Army engaged in an orgy of terror, intimidating a horrified population.

The newly freed Bishop of Veszprém, just as soon as he could get about in a one-horse carriage with his secretary driving, traveled throughout his devastated diocese, bringing his people consolation and hope, and strengthening their will to live.

On one of these pastoral visits in the summer of 1945, he made a detour to visit his home town and tell his elderly parents the entire story of his second imprisonment. His father was then 81 and his mother was 71.

CHAPTER 5

Manning the Fortresses

When the Nazis finally released Bishop Mindszenty from
prison, he walked from Sopronkőhida to Pápa with his fellow
ex-prisoner, Louis Shvoy, Bishop of Székesfehérvár. At
Pápa they separated and Bishop Mindszenty stopped to visit
an official whom he had helped to liberate from a Nazi
concentration camp the previous year, Mayor Donald Sulyok.[1] The Bishop hoped that Sulyok might get him some
kind of vehicle for the rest of the long journey home.

Mayor Sulyok, however, knowing what atrocities were
being committed on all the roads by the Red Army, felt
strongly that the Bishop of Veszprém should not travel alone,
and suggested that he ask for a car and military escort
from the Soviet commanding officer in the city.

"A Hungarian Bishop cannot ask a favor from the Soviet
Army," Bishop Mindszenty replied. He simply could not in
conscience ask a favor from the agent of the atheist forces
whose main goal was to destroy the Church.

Bishop Mindszenty had studied history well, and he
knew that whenever Church leaders compromised with the
Church's persecutors, the persecutors were strengthened and
their power prolonged. "New persecutors of the Church are
replacing the old ones," he had written in 1942. "Swollen
with pride at their whirlwind victories, they are temporarily
on top; but the Church always outlives them."[2]

At the end of World War II, the Nazi persecutors of
the Church were replaced by the atheistic Bolsheviks. Following in the footsteps of the conquering Red Army, Hungarian Communists spread all over the country. The same
men who had escaped to the Soviet Union after the collapse
of their brief despotic rule in 1919, now returned to Hungary
with the Red Army to build a "people's republic" in the
Soviet pattern.

On December 21, 1944, the Communists organized a provisional National Assembly at Debrecen in eastern Hungary, which had just been occupied by the Russian army. Without any elections, the following deputies were appointed to office: 72 Communists, 57 Smallholders Party members, 35 Social Democrats, 12 Peasant Party members, 19 union representatives, and 35 independents. The same day, a provisional coalition Cabinet was established with two ministers each from the Communist, Social Democrat and Smallholders Parties and one from the Peasant Party. Under Russian orders, the new Communist puppet regime also put three generals and a count in the Cabinet to give the West the illusion of a representative government.

The executive and judicial branches of the Government were put under the control of the four parties. In every county, city and town, the existing administrative and governmental institutions were ordered replaced by national committees manned by agents of the four major parties and the labor unions. Since not only the Communist Party, but also the Social Democrat and Peasant Parties and all the labor unions, were under the actual influence of the Bolsheviks, all administrative actions and all court rulings were carried out according to Communist dictate.

The Provisional Government had one important duty: to plan and organize a Communist-controlled parliamentary election for the autumn of 1945. In the spring of 1945, all Government offices were moved from Debrecen to Budapest and an election campaign got underway.

The Marxists' goal was, first of all, to organize the population into the four-party framework established in Debrecen. The Communist secret police played an essential role in assuring Marxist domination of all the major parties. Exactly like the brutal Soviet NKVD, the Hungarian secret police carried out sadistic persecutions throughout the country which subjected the population to a reign of terror. These secret police agents were cruel and immoral types recruited from the criminal underworld. Among them were many who had previously played sadistic roles as Nazi stormtroopers. The new Government callously released from

prison even the most dangerous criminals if they would join
the Communist Party and do its bidding.

The Communists' main goal was to eliminate every courageous statesman and talented politician who would not
cooperate with them. Simultaneously, they used agents and
informers to cause discord and dissension among non-Communist political and social groups. They were successful in
this objective even among Catholics because they cleverly
made use of a few so-called "progressive Catholics."

The Communists organized a group of such "progressive
Catholics," starting in Debrecen. This group included some
inexperienced young men craving for political advancement
and several neurotic priests. At first, they were only pressed
to make innocent statements about "the necessity of cooperation between Marxists and Christians in a time of un-
precedented national disaster." Later, they were used to
weaken the unity of the Church and to diminish its resistance
to the accelerated Communist anti-religious activities. These
"progressive Catholics" were of significant help to the Communists in carrying out their evil objectives. Among the
progressive Catholic intellectuals who moved to Budapest
after the war were the priests, László Bánáss and Stephen
Balogh, and a university professor named Julius Szekfű.

The collaboration of such leftist Catholics caused trouble
immediately. The leaders of the KALOT movement (Catholic Farmers Association) drifted toward cooperation with the
Communists because of their tactical error in joining the
Levente movement during World War II. Jesuit Fathers
Eugene Kerkai and Töhötöm Nagy were the KALOT's
two dynamic leaders who arranged the unification. The entire teaching faculty of the Szombathely Seminary had unanimously asked Father Kerkai to refuse the invitation to merge
with the Levente movement. Those familiar with the internal
affairs of the KALOT, however, knew that the hot-headed
Father Töhötöm Nagy was the one really responsible for
this merger. Inexperienced and stubborn, he had his eye on
only one problem: how to solve the KALOT's financial
troubles. His solution was Government subsidy.

An even more serious blunder resulted from Father

Töhötöm Nagy's political naivete. On his own initiative, at the end of 1944 he went to the Russians and offered to cooperate with them if they would not dissolve the KALOT. The Hungarian Communists had previously declared their intention to dissolve all "Fascist" organizations, an epithet by which they meant to include the KALOT and Levente movements. When the Russians saw that the KALOT, a farmer-youth organization, had a very large membership and could not be easily controlled politically, they eagerly accepted Father Nagy's offer.

From that time on, the KALOT leaders had lost their independence. They had to follow Russian demands in their planning and activities. These demands were, of course, always in the interest of the Communists. The threat of dissolution was the sword of Damocles hanging over their heads.

I first heard the authentic details of this situation from Bishop Mindszenty while spending a day with him in his native village in June 1945. He told me how Father Töhötöm Nagy, acting in the name of the KALOT, had rejected the idea of the formation of an independent Christian Party which the Bishops favored. Instead, Father Nagy at Debrecen committed himself and the KALOT to support the Smallholders Party. Catholics, therefore, were left with only the Smallholders Party to support.

Confronted by this situation, the Bishops would have liked to have replaced the weak and inexperienced leaders of the Smallholders Party with stronger and more able politicians, and they urged the KALOT leaders to make these changes. At any other time, this change in personnel could have been accomplished rather easily since a victory by the Smallholders Party depended completely on the KALOT's nationwide network of well-trained organizers. The KALOT leaders, however, knew that to accede to the Bishops' request meant that the KALOT movement would be dissolved by the Communists.

By his shortsighted political maneuvering, Father Töhötöm Nagy allowed the KALOT to become more and more controlled by the Communists. Finally, local groups aban-

doned it in such great numbers that this farmer-youth organization, which had previously shown such great promise
of being politically important in Hungary, came to its tragic
end.[3]

In the midst of this turmoil, Pope Pius XII appointed
Joseph Mindszenty Archbishop of Esztergom and Primate
of the Catholic Church in Hungary. Cardinal Serédi had
died in the first days of the Russian occupation of Esztergom,
and the Russians had expelled the Papal Nuncio from the
country in March 1945. There had been no contact between
the Hungarian Bishops' Conference and Rome for nearly
six months, and Bishop Mindszenty was administering the
Sacrament of Confirmation in Pápa when finally informed
of his appointment.

"The Catholic Church does not hide when a storm is
gathering, but is everywhere with and for the Hungarian
people. It does not seek temporal, but only divine, protection."[4] These first words of Archbishop Mindszenty as the
new Primate of Hungary, spoken at Pápa to his well-wishers,
were characteristic of the man and indicated that he clearly
understood his difficult mission at that crisis in history.

In his inaugural address, Archbishop Mindszenty spoke
even more forthrightly: "Bleeding Hungary is drowning in
the maelstrom of the worst moral, legal and economic collapse in our history. Our psalm is the *De Profundis;* our
prayer is the *Miserere;* our prophet is Jeremiah; our world is
the *Apocalypse.* We sit at the waters of Babylon and captors
try to teach us alien songs. ... I want to be a good shepherd
who, if necessary, will give his life for his sheep, for the
Church and our homeland."[5]

The new Primate knew only too well both the theory and
the reality of Communism, and its cunning and deceitful
tactics. Beginning in 1919, he had continuously and thor-

oughly studied every phase of the persecution of the Church in Russia. He knew that compromise had failed to secure any freedom for the Church there. He knew the tragic case of the Russian Orthodox Patriarch Tikhon and his successor, the more "diplomatic" Metropolitan Sergei.

Archbishop Mindszenty understood that in Russia a diabolical atheistic power had confronted the leaders of the Orthodox Church. He had written years before: "Hell has never before mobilized such power. An officially atheistic dictatorship, with $5\frac{1}{2}$ million atheist Communist agents, fight unitedly and relentlessly with red-hot hatred against God, religion and the Church. They carry on their fight in the schools, radio, newspapers, literature, the theater, art, advertisements, cartoons, and caricatures, and even through robberies and sacrileges in the churches."[6]

In his inaugural speech he exhorted: "Let the nation storm Heaven with prayers now! If we begin to really pray again, we will gain renewed strength and confidence. My trust is in a campaign of prayers by millions of the faithful, and in my mother's Rosary, now held even more tightly in her hands."[7]

Joseph Mindszenty took the Archbishop's chair in Esztergom (on the northern border of Hungary) on October 7, 1945, and with it a monumental workload few prelates in the world could match. Construction of new religious buildings was hardly feasible in a country now devastated and impoverished. The material needs of his people were so great that he had to move quickly with the most diversified apostolic works.

First, he took care of his own Archdiocese which included the city of Budapest. He made long and tiresome trips for on-the-spot inspections of parishes with particular difficulties, to organize help and evaluate local possibilities. Much time had to be spent in the capital where 700,000

Catholics lived. He made frequent speeches in the Budapest churches and at the festivals and meetings of various organizations. The Primate's house in Budapest was largely in ruins, but it still had a couple of usable rooms. He told his friends, "It is fitting that the Primate of a devastated country live in a devastated house."

His prime concern was to help the needy and persecuted. He worked rapidly to reorganize Catholic charities in the capital and throughout the country. In the first few years of his new office, he went to Rome twice and researched every possibility for obtaining material aid for his people. Hungarian Catholic charities obtained the most help from the Bishops' Conference of the United States and from the Catholics in Belgium.

At Christmastime, Archbishop Mindszenty started a relief program with the slogan "A parcel for our starving brothers in Budapest." He issued a pastoral letter asking every Catholic to join in the work of Catholic charities. In another appeal, he described the desperate conditions of the Hungarian people. "This winter brings critical shortages in food and clothing for hundreds of thousands of our people. Hunger can be tolerated by strong men for days, but not by our old people, children and babies. In these times, even the hardy have little strength!"[8]

He visited the packed concentration camps in and around Budapest where the victims of the new Communist tyranny were eking out a pitiful existence. It was for these unfortunate people that he appealed in his first pastoral letter as Primate:

"There are many who have been deprived of the basic right of personal liberty and who have been held in concentration camps for months without even being told why, without any court trial or sentence, sometimes without even being questioned. We raise our voice in protest now, at the beginning of winter, because we fear increased shortages in food and clothing. We ask the authorities to recognize their responsibility before God and history, to ease the terrible suffering of Hungarians, and to shore up the sea of sorrow which has swept over so many families."[9]

As the Catholic leader of Hungary, Archbishop Mindszenty did not swerve from his chief pastoral obligation to lead souls to their eternal salvation. He kept in constant personal contact not only with the clergy of his own Archdiocese but from all parts of the country. He often attended meetings and conferences of the clergy, and his directives were always enthusiastically accepted.

He urged everyone to live a deeply pious life and he inaugurated a spiritual revival among clergy and people: a movement of prayer and atonement. He consistently set a good example himself. In monastic simplicity, he devoted himself exclusively to prayer and work. He slept very little and worked most of the night. (Even in his youth, he had seemed to get along on four or five hours of sleep a night.) He ate the simplest food. His priests often secretly mixed vitamins in his soup to prevent damage to his health from so much fasting.

In another pastoral letter to the Hungarian people, Archbishop Mindszenty announced the necessity for a spiritual crusade of prayer, saying: "Human strength alone is not enough for man to live and progress. Man's struggle is in vain if not joined by God's blessing. ... We put all our hope in the Hearts of Jesus and Mary. From them we ask for and hope to gain salvation."[10]

During this nationwide novena, the Catholic churches everywhere were filled. Archbishop Mindszenty concluded the novena on February 10, 1946 with a ceremony at the Church of Perpetual Adoration in Budapest. Huge crowds in the streets outside listened through loudspeakers to his sermon.

The Communists were infuriated by the success of the novena. When Archbishop Mindszenty left the church to the enthusiastic applause of tens of thousands, Communist *agents provocateurs* mixed through the crowd and began to cheer the late Hungarian Nazi leader Szálasi. The police appeared immediately and arrested many persons leaving the Church as Nazi demonstrators.

The next day the Communists organized a noisy demonstration in the streets of Budapest. Milling in the midst of

Pope Pius XII confers the insignia of the Cardinalate on Joseph Mindszenty, February 19, 1946.

◀ **Cardinal Mindszenty arriving at the Vatican.** On the right is his secretary, Father Andrew Zakar.

quiet, orderly crowds of unemployed workers, paid agents yelled at the top of their voices: "We want work and bread — and a rope for Mindszenty!" The Marxist news media reported immediately that the "anti-proletarian" attitude of the Primate had provoked the workers' "spontaneous" protest.

In February 1946, Pope Pius XII elevated Archbishop Mindszenty to the Cardinalate. Great crowds of people greeted him in the basilica of Vác where the new Cardinal gave his first sermon after returning from Rome.

During the next few weeks, Lenten retreats and missions were held in every parish. Even more men participated than women! At Easter, the Catholic newspaper *Hungarian Courier* reported: "Three-fourths of the faithful present in the cathedrals, churches and chapels were men. This year, approximately 38 per cent more men were present at sermons and 51 percent more at processions than last year."[11]

The success of this spiritual revival was also shown by the participation on May 5, 1946 of more than 100,000 men in a ten-mile pilgrimage personally led by Cardinal Mindszenty walking from Budapest to the shrine of Máriaremete. On August 20, some 500,000 men participated in a magnificent religious procession which he organized.

When the other bishops saw how Cardinal Mindszenty's sermons brought a new religious spirit to the Catholics in Budapest, they invited him more and more often to speak in their own dioceses on holydays. The Bishop of Székesfehérvár was the first to invite him, and in "Red Csepel," a Marxist stronghold, 10,000 workers greeted him and overflowed the churches.

During the summer of 1946, Cardinal Mindszenty gave sermons to 10,000 Catholics in Kalocsa and Sopron. On September 8, he led a pilgrimage to Máriapócs where he spoke to 250,000 pilgrims. A week later, 20,000 of the faithful heard him at Zalaegerszeg. On September 22, he addressed a huge crowd at Szeged for the 900th anniversary of the martyrdom of St. Gerard. Here he answered the local Bishop's greeting with these words, "In all humility, I look upon myself as merely a servant of the nation and of my people. I want to fulfill this service, whatever the price."[12]

On the morning of October 20, he spoke to a huge crowd at Pécs, and in the evening to a large group of Catholic parents. On November 30, he appeared in Debrecen, the citadel of Hungarian Calvinism, where the city's Protestant chief warden welcomed him with these words: "We greet the first pontiff of our brothers in Christianity in the Hungarian Fatherland — not with mere politeness, but with genuine love and fellowship."[13]

In the first half of 1947, Cardinal Mindszenty preached to tens of thousands of pilgrims at Győr, Székesfehérvár, Szentgotthárd, Budafok, Dombóvár, and Hatvan. From June 11 to July 11, he went to Canada to participate in the Marian Congress there. He took this opportunity to visit several Hungarian parishes in Canada and the United States, and he used this trip effectively to collect donations for his impoverished people.

During those years, I was often a guest at the Cardinal's mother's home in Mindszent. When he would take a few days of rest at her home, he would give his personal secretaries a vacation and ask me to come over from nearby Szombathely (where I was a professor of theology) and serve as his secretary pro tem. His mother regularly read the two Catholic weekly newspapers, *New Man* and *Sacred Heart News,* in which she followed her son's nationwide activities. She told me how she asked God every day for His blessing on her son's apostolic work.

After reading about the success of Cardinal Mindszenty's apostolic travels and the huge audiences he attracted,

Stefano Rotondo, Cardinal Mindszenty's titular church in Rome.

Cardinal Mindszenty at the 1947 Marian Congress in Canada.

the reader may be curious to know what drew these large
crowds to him. The usual "religio-sociological" reasons may
partially account for this phenomenon. After a disastrous
war has been lost and life is so very difficult, men turn to
God in larger numbers and tend to listen to their consciences
more readily.

But this circumstance alone cannot possibly explain the
tremendous religious revival which took place in Hungary.
The person about whom such a remarkable movement crys-
tallizes must possess genuine charisma or other extraordinary
abilities. In the case of Cardinal Mindszenty, the words of
Bishop Rogács are particularly pertinent. In welcoming the
Cardinal on September 8, 1947 in the presence of the Bishops' Conference and a large gathering of priests, he declared:

"We are grateful for the guidance Your Eminence has
given us, both personally and in the name of the Bishops'
Conference. Your charismatic wisdom leads hesitant minds
along the right way, gives strength to weary souls and fortitude to those who have abandoned hope. Possessing the
steadfastness of a St. Ambrose, you are the Rock to which
the Hungarian people, both Catholic and non-Catholic, cling
in order not to be swept away by the waves."[14]

In addition to his sanctity and the apostolic enthusiasm
of a soul always prepared for martyrdom, the crowds were
also attracted by his impressive oratorical talents. He always
had good rapport with his audiences and chose the theme
and tone of his speeches with discretion. A good example of
the way he could inspire his listeners was the speech he
delivered at Szentgotthárd. His mother and I were among
the 15,000 who listened with rapt attention and devotion, as
the Cardinal spoke with fiery emphasis:

"In the past, great fortresses stood watch over our people in the Hungarian countryside. This area was watched,
defended, and secured by the fortresses of Németújvár,
Szalónak, Körmend, and Csáktornya. Those fortresses now
belong to the hoary past; only legends and the tangled vines
clinging to their ruins still tell of ancient functions, forgotten memories, and days of past glory.

"We cannot live without fortresses even today. Thank

God we have fortresses for our defense: the Church of our native land, our Catholic schools, the fundamental unit of the family, and the hallowed cemeteries of our beloved dead.

"What the heart is to a man's life, so is the Church to the life of a city or village. The Church is the House of God and the Gate of Heaven. *(Genesis 28:17)*. This House of God is the home of prayer and the sacred place for receiving Holy Communion. It is a divine fortress for souls; its beauty reflects the magnificence of the community of believers who share in the Precious Blood of the Lamb of God.

"Each church building is sanctified by the prayers of Holy Mother Church and the presence of the Body and Blood of Jesus. It is sanctified continuously throughout the centuries by the piety of the faithful — by their Baptisms, Confessions, Holy Communions, the nuptial Masses of their parents, grandparents, great-grandparents and distant ancestors. When we enter our churches, let the presence of God penetrate our souls. Let us reflect with awe on the prayers of our ancestors in this holy place, and the traces of their footprints on its worn stones.

"A saintly twin of the Church itself is the Catholic school. It may indeed be said that the school originated at the altar of the Church. When our first King, St. Stephen, ordered a church for every ten villages, in effect he also gave schools to the Hungarian people. When no one else cared about education, it was at and near the altar, pulpit, and baptismal fountain of our churches that our ancestors learned the alphabet, arithmetic, agriculture, and industrial skills, in addition to their religion.

"When the faithful multiplied and the school left the church building, it did not go far away. Our national tradition is that the Gospels and the school are the two stone tablets enshrining the covenant of the Hungarian people. Either the school will instruct in the spirit of the Church to help produce saintly souls, or it will become a workshop of evil, corrupted and corrupting. History teaches us that, as the school moves farther away from the Church, it goes closer to the world of jails, concentration camps, sin and damnation. The school must be the home of virtue and science. If virtue is not taught in it, God save us from its science!

"Our third fortress is the family hearth, beside which, in accordance with God's law and blessing, generations follow generations. Each member of the family receives his status and value from on high: the father from the Divine Father, the mother from the Blessed Virgin, and the children from the Divine Child, Jesus. In a devout family, each of the faithful sees in the other the face of Him who is the Divine Authority. When they come to pray together at the family table, they radiate the light of the Holy Family.

"Therefore, holy are the father and mother who reflect the Family of Nazareth: an eternal crown awaits them and their children, and blessed is the entire nation.

"The family is a wonderfully strong fortress if it remains linked to the sacred world of the Church and the Catholic school. These three together are indeed our fortresses. We must live in, watch over, and struggle to preserve these fortresses of the faith until God calls us to our eternal rest.

"The cemetery is God's meadow for countless generations, a hallowed place to sleep and rest in the Lord until the trumpet of the Last Judgment sounds and the bodies of the faithful rejoin their souls in the glorious Resurrection of Easter.

"Whether our cemeteries be full of beautiful marble memorials or stately oak and acacia trees, the presence of our first three fortresses hovers over the ashes of our beloved ones. As from the pulpit of the Church, the school desk of the Catholic school, and the ancestral hearth, the graves of our dead cry out always to the world of the living: 'Children, do not forget the message of the previous generations – be faithful to your fortresses.'

"Amidst the storms and tempests which sweep our world today, eternally holy be the Church, the Catholic school and the family home. Stand guard – hold fast at their thresholds!"[15]

Cardinal Mindszenty further stimulated the religious life of his people by announcing a Marian year in honor of the Virgin Mary. The devotion of Hungarian Catholics to Mary dates from their first King, St. Stephen, who consecrated his country and his celebrated Crown (which the Pope had given him) to the Holy Virgin. Ever since, Hungarians have called Mary the "Queen of Hungary," and the feast of the Assumption of Mary on August 15 was celebrated every year with a special ceremony. Cardinal Mindszenty announced and opened the "Year of Our Lady of Hungary" in Esztergom in the presence of the Bishops' Conference and 60,000 Catholics on August 15, 1947.

From then on, everywhere in the country, special Marydays were held, particularly in the larger towns and at important shrines. In Csongrád, for example, 70,000 Catholics gathered. According to the newspaper *Hungarian Courier,* on August 15 and September 8, 1947 three million pilgrims gathered in the nation's various Marian shrines to attend liturgical services. On September 8, there were 100,000 pilgrims at Szombathely. On September 14, the Primate again led a penitential pilgrimage of 100,000 men who walked from Budapest to Máriaremete. On September 20, 120,000 believers attended Cardinal Mindszenty's Mass and sermon. Between October 4 and 7, a Marian Congress was held in Budapest at which a youth assembly attracted 150,000 boys and girls; the meeting for workers drew 80,000. The Sunday High Mass and main session attracted 250,000, and the next day 200,000 participated in a session for parents.[16]

Whenever possible, the Cardinal prayed with the pilgrims. During 1948, he celebrated Mass and delivered sermons at 12 Marian Congresses held in various cities and towns. These successful Marian Congresses were acutely embarrassing to the Communists. They did not dare to forbid the "Year of Our Lady of Hungary," but they tried to hinder and upset its ceremonies in every possible way.

They refused to issue railroad tickets to pilgrims who wanted to take trains to Marian celebrations. The number of trains and railway cars on those routes was often decreased. Trucks were requisitioned to prevent people from

using them, and horses were "inspected" by officials to keep
people from using their carriages. Traffic in entire counties
was often prohibited on the pretense of fictitious epidemics.
The Communist bureaucrats often shut off water and power
facilities to harass the religious gatherings, or prohibited the
installation of public address systems, or declared that an
"accidental power failure" prevented their use. Tractors
with noisy engines were raced near churches and shrines
when Masses and sermons were going on.

State officials were often fired for participating in religious pilgrimages. At other times, the police used their clubs
to disperse religious processions such as those at the Cave
Church in Budapest on June 13, 1948 and in Celldömölk
on September 12, 1948.

In spite of all these harassments, Catholic Action leaders
proudly reported at the end of the "Year of Our Lady of Hungary" that more than 4½ million of the faithful had participated in the various Marian celebrations and pilgrimages.[17]

The Communists were even more vexed by the Cardinal's
skillful administration of Church affairs. They were frus-
trated at their failure either to intimidate him with terroristic tactics or to mislead him by their wily methods. Their
efforts failed not only because of the Cardinal's steadfastness of purpose, but also because, as a scholarly historian,
he was thoroughly familiar with the methods the Soviets
had used to persecute the Church ever since 1918.

He had a complete knowledge of the literature describing the inhuman tactics used by the Russian Bolsheviks to
crush the Ukrainian Catholic Church after World War. II.
He had studied the writings of Marx and Lenin. He knew
that the Communists are deadly serious about implementing
the Marxist-Leninist thesis that all religion is the instrument

of the "reactionary bourgeoisie" and therefore must be liqui-
dated as soon as this is practical.

Cardinal Mindszenty, of course, was also familiar with
Lenin's corollary that the Communist Party is authorized to
"occasionally subordinate anti-religious activities to its main
goal." The cunning Lenin had instructed the Party that, in
certain cases where priests and religious believers could be
persuaded to join and work for Communist fronts, Party
members were to conceal their militant atheism.

At first, the Hungarian Communists followed this prag-
matic strategy devised by Lenin. While they waged a merci-
less war against the middle class, they cautiously avoided
attacking the religious feelings of the people. Even the
ruthless Red Army was under orders to be circumspect in
dealing with religious personnel and organizations.

At the very beginning of the Communist takeover of
Hungary, the Party ordered its local cells to help in the
reconstruction of religious buildings, its cadres to attend
religious services and processions while wearing Communist
Party insignia, and its members to try to establish friendly
relationships with the clergy. This stratagem fooled a few
inexperienced priests who declared themselves pleased with
the Communists' "piety."

While publicly asserting their good will toward the
Church, the Communists struck three major blows against it:
(1) They stripped religious organizations, institutions and
schools of their financial support. (2) They closed down all
Church newspapers, periodicals and magazines by refusing
permits and limiting newsprint. (3) They cleverly prevented
any political parties of Christian orientation and ideology
from running candidates in Parliamentary elections.

The Communists justified these radical measures against
the Church as necessary "to restore social order" after a
disastrous war. They used the same reason to justify their
expulsion of the Papal Nuncio soon after the Red Army
entered Hungary.

Cardinal Mindszenty, of course, treated these pre-planned
measures against the Church as grave violations of the right
to freedom of religion. He often raised his voice to protest

the way the Church was restricted in the expression of its
religious and social doctrine by being deprived of its own
daily newspaper. Several times he officially called upon the
Government to comply with the Agrarian Reform Law which
promised compensation for expropriated Church lands.
Speakers at Catholic rallies and meetings would point out
that Catholics made up more than two-thirds of the Hungarian population, but did not have any representation in
the Parliament because of the Communists' dictatorial ma-
nipulation of the Party system.

In the national election of November 4, 1945, the elec-
torate could vote only for candidates of political parties permitted by the Allied Control Committee. This Committee
was controlled by the Commander of Russian troops in
Hungary, General Voroshilov.[18] Permission was granted only
to those parties already represented in the Provisional Parliament, which were the several Marxist parties and the one
non-Marxist party, the Smallholders Party. Catholics felt
obliged to support the Smallholders Party even though they
had no voice in selecting its leaders. When this Party won
the election with a 57.7 per cent majority, its weak leaders
were successfully pressured by the Russians to divide the
ministerial portfolios fifty-fifty with the Communists. Of
course, the Communists made sure that they got the Ministry of the Interior which had charge of the secret police.

The Communists took advantage of this coalition Government to put through a policy designed to weaken the
Church even further. They proceeded to ban Catholic youth
organizations, prohibit religious education, and secularize the
Catholic schools.

In spite of the deteriorating political situation, Cardinal
Mindszenty struggled successfully for nearly four years to
defend Church organizations, religious education programs,
and Catholic schools against the accelerating Communist
policy of false propaganda and terroristic harassment.[19]

In the fall of 1947, the Communists increased their power
in the coalition Government by means of fraudulent and
falsified elections and by brutal persecution of opposition
parties. This new Communist "coalition" Government or-

dered the expropriation of all Catholic schools on June 16, 1948, a measure which caused fierce popular resentment. In this war of nerves, Cardinal Mindszenty continued his vigorous defense of the schools and organized a nationwide protest. It was obvious that this confiscation of the Catholic schools by the Communist Government was against the wishes of the overwhelming majority of the Hungarian people, and this was so reported by Western news agencies.[20]

It was during this bitter struggle over the Catholic schools that the decision was made in Moscow and Budapest to silence Cardinal Mindszenty.

Cardinal Mindszenty. This photograph shows an etching made in 1947 by Carl Lünsdorf.

CHAPTER 6

The Gathering Storm

During the summer of 1948 everyone was nervous and edgy. The expropriation of the Catholic schools and the introduction of required courses in Marxism in all schools alarmed the entire population. Parents were terribly concerned about the atheistic and Marxist indoctrination forced upon their children.

On the other hand, the new Communist bosses were apprehensive about the popular reaction to their policies. It was completely obvious that the overwhelming majority of the Hungarian people wanted a religious education for their children and opposed the expropriation of the private schools. Everyone could see that the enforcement of this law passed by the Communist pseudo-Parliament was a clear violation of repeated public promises made by the Communists that any new "reforms" would be passed by "legal" means alone and "according to the consent of the people."

The Communists were surprised at the popular resistance, and even more by Western interest in Hungarian affairs. This was the first time that the Free World received prompt and detailed information about anti-religious actions behind the Iron Curtain.

Cardinal Mindszenty regularly submitted documentation to the various news agencies, especially the Catholic press services, so that newspapers and radio stations throughout the world could expose the Communist lies. The West was thus rather well informed about the religious persecution in Hungary, and the Western press severely criticized the Communist moves to wipe out religious freedom. News of this religious persecution in Hungary broke simultaneously with the Communist plot against the democratic Government in Czechoslovakia. World opinion turned against Communism, and anti-Communist voices in the Free World were encouraged to speak.

The Communists knew that it was to their interest to mask their anti-religious tactics in Eastern Europe and to avoid a public confrontation between Church and State. The Hungarian Bolsheviks caught on quickly to the fact that, so long as Cardinal Mindszenty headed the Catholic Church in Hungary, the forcible stamping out of religion would mean a life-and-death struggle between Church and State. The Primate always vigorously and publicly exposed the anti-religious tactics of the Communists.

Despite many attempts to get him to "cooperate," the Communists simply could not divert him from his vigorous defense of religious freedom. They were just as unsuccessful with their tactics of intimidation. They were only too well aware of the fact that Cardinal Mindszenty was the Hungarian standard-bearer in the conflict over private schools, and that he was giving the facts about this struggle to the foreign press.

The Cardinal's courageous resistance, coupled with increased world interest in Hungarian affairs and the Communists' fear of an open break with the Church, all combined to bring about a change of Communist Party tactics during the summer of 1948. The top Hungarian Communists reached a consensus that the only way to avoid a violent struggle between Church and State was to eliminate Cardinal Mindszenty from his leadership position. Henceforth, all anti-religious attacks were aimed specifically at the person of Cardinal Mindszenty.

The Communist officials and their controlled press and radio hammered away at the "anti-democratic" attitude of the Cardinal, labeling him an "enemy of the people." They repeated *ad nauseam* that Cardinal Mindszenty refused to "recognize" the Republic; that he was organizing a "revolution" to overthrow it; that he "obstinately" opposed peaceful relations between Church and State by demanding the return of Church properties; and that he was "causing irreparable harm" not only to the Hungarian Republic, but to the whole Catholic Church!

Here is how Cardinal Mindszenty replied to these accusations: "The trouble does not lie in my peaceful or unpeaceful dispositions. . . . Not everything is peaceful which is called peace. The cloak of peace and justice is desirable, but the question is, who actually wears this mantle? The means of peace are not belligerent. Peace does not bring the fruits of war: injustice, cruelty, vengeance, unjust deportations, and forced labor. These are not the marks of peace, but of hatred and violence. Every new bishop is admonished at his consecration: 'Don't turn light into darkness, or darkness into light; don't call error truth; don't call evil good, or good evil.' To this I would add, don't call it peace if it is not peace!"[1]

The Communists increased the number of secret police who followed the Cardinal everywhere in order to put his trusted friends and co-workers under surveillance. A whole army of secret agents spread over the country to investigate every place where the Cardinal had worked during three decades. Their object was to find something in the Cardinal's past with which they could compromise him. By blackmail and intimidation, the secret police succeeded in getting slanderous statements against him from a few cowards with unsavory reputations. The newspapers published these slanders and they were eagerly reiterated over the radio.

The public, however, was by this time alert to the customary Communist tactic of broadcasting trumped-up charges against their enemies. Consequently, this campaign of vilification was counterproductive. Not only Catholics, but every decent Hungarian, rejoiced in the fact that, in spite of a searching investigation of his more than 30 years of priestly ministry, the Communists could not dig up the slightest evidence to compromise the Cardinal. The Communist attacks merely enhanced the Cardinal's prestige, and the whole nation now shared a concern for his fate.

One indication of the anxiety the people felt and their fear that the Cardinal might be subjected to Communist vengeance was the substantial growth in the volume of his daily mail. Another was the increase in the crowds of people who surrounded him wherever he went. The Szombathely Cathedral was always filled when he appeared, and overflow crowds outside listened to his voice over the loudspeaker, applauding him vigorously when he departed.

Cardinal Mindszenty was well aware of the danger to which he was exposed. This is why his sermons included the recurring theme that a pastor must serve his flock even at the cost of his own life. When he consecrated Bishop Francis Rogács in the Szombathely Cathedral on June 29, 1948, the Cardinal's sermon included these words about the role of the Church:

"Throughout the world, the battle rages between spiritual and worldly weapons, between conscience and the sword. . . . The secular power is ill at ease in the presence of God, and even in the presence of the Church which represents Almighty God and the spiritual freedom He has given us. It is an everlasting blessing that there is Someone who indicates, even to the most powerful, what is right and what is wrong. What becomes of nations when truth is silenced?"

Turning to the newly-consecrated Bishop, Cardinal Mindszenty added, "Your vocation is to proclaim the voice of conscience, just as we prayed today. Don't call light darkness, nor the darkness, light; don't call evil good, or good evil."[2]

After the ceremony, the Cardinal called me and asked me to go with him to Mindszent and to substitute for his regular secretary for about a week. The Cardinal intended to take a badly-needed rest at his mother's home. The struggle for the Catholic schools had taxed his physical strength to the limit and had exhausted the stamina of the other Chancery officials. The Cardinal looked terribly tired, and I learned later that he had agreed to take this brief rest only after strict orders from his doctor.

The Cardinal's secretary, Father Andrew Zakar, had been on the go day and night, and his urgent need of a rest was obvious. He planned to go to the Cistercian Monastery in Borsodpuszta in the Bakony Hills.

About four o'clock, Cardinal Mindszenty, Father Zakar and I drove to Mindszent. No one except Mother Mindszenty knew we were coming. She waited for us at the front window and hurried to open the gate when she heard the car. She gave her son such a joyful embrace that she did not notice until we were inside the house how much weight he had lost. After inviting us to be seated, she said anxiously, "Joseph, you look so thin and so tired, and I know you are worn out from all your problems and cares. A few peaceful days here at home will be good for you."

Mother Mindszenty served us an afternoon snack of ham, cold cuts, and cake. When she asked what we wanted to drink, Father Zakar and I asked for tea. The Cardinal said he preferred a little drink from the vineyard of Mindszent. After the tea and wine were served, the Cardinal raised his glass with a twinkle in his eye and asked, "Mother, how did it happen that this homemade wine has no barrel odor?"

Mother Mindszenty explained that this was a little family joke. Once long ago, when in a big hurry, she had put her best wine in an old moldy barrel, which gave it such a terrible taste that she had to borrow wine from a neighbor to serve all her guests until the next grape harvest.

After we enjoyed our refreshments, the Cardinal asked his mother, "Why didn't you come to the Bishop's consecration in Szombathely?" "Because they didn't send a car for me, as they promised," she replied.

Cardinal Mindszenty looked at me, and I lamely explained that the last week had been so hectic because of the expropriation of the Catholic schools that this was surely the reason why the car had been forgotten.

Mother Mindszenty was not offended, saying graciously, "I can understand that. No one should feel hurt at being forgotten in such a topsy-turvy world. I was present at the consecration of *three* Bishops — when Cardinal Serédi consecrated you and the Bishops of Csanád and Szombathely."

The Cardinal urged Father Zakar to spend the next few days in total rest so that plenty of sleep and walks in the woods would erase all worries from his mind. He left after

Cardinal Mindszenty's Mother. This photograph was taken September 8, 1947 at the closing procession of a three-day Marian Congress in Szombathely.

he had finished his tea, and we promised to pick him up in a week at the Monastery in Borsodpuszta.

From where I was sitting, I had a good view of the street through a front window. My attention was attracted to two young men who were riding a bicycle back and forth. Every now and then, they would slow down in front of the house, ride closer to the window and look in. A third man, leaning against the fence, was also eyeing us closely.

I knew almost everyone in town, and so I knew these men were strangers. The obvious deduction was that they were secret police. I wasn't sure, however, because the secret police had never before made its surveillance so blatant. On the Cardinal's previous visits to Mindszent, the municipal or school officials would suddenly have an "unexpected supervisor" who would remain as long as the Cardinal did. But these "supervisors" had always been discreet in concealing that their real mission was to monitor the Primate.

The presence of these strangers in the street disturbed me, and I wanted to find out how and when they had arrived in town. I excused myself on the pretext of wanting to go to church and finish my breviary. I left through the orchard to avoid being seen and called on a nearby neighbor who had a clever and intelligent teenage son. I asked the boy to do a little cautious detective work. We agreed to meet in an hour at the bowling alley in the parish courtyard. Then I went on to church.

An hour later, we met where the usual Sunday afternoon bowling game was in full swing. After some pleasantries with the bowlers, the boy gave me his report. He said that six newcomers had arrived in the village by bicycle, trying to create the impression that they were tourists from a distant town. His friends were all convinced that the strangers were secret police agents sent to watch the Cardinal. The lad assured me that he and his friends would keep a close eye on the strangers, watch our house throughout the night, and let me know of any change in their behavior.

I left to discuss with the local pastor the Mass schedule for the next day. It then occurred to me that I had neglected to ask the Cardinal what time he wanted to say Mass, so I invited the pastor back to Mother Mindszenty's home.

When we arrived, we found the Cardinal in the center of a crowd of children who were all sons and daughters and grandchildren of various members of his family. He always talked with these children when he visited Mindszent. He knew all their names, even the toddlers. He talked to them about their studies, their games, and their good times. He quizzed the older children about their report cards. Then he opened his big suitcase and delighted every child with a small gift: books, tablets, pencils, medals, toys or candies.

The children left when Mother Mindszenty announced supper and the Cardinal remarked: "Every priest is happy when his own relatives reject the fashion of limiting the size of their families to one child. He can then preach with greater conviction about the sins against the unborn. Children are always a blessing, even in these perilous times."

After deciding the next morning's Mass schedule, the pastor left and we had supper on the porch. We started with light conversation, but soon became serious. Cardinal Mindszenty's mother brought up the charges which the radio and newspapers were hurling against her son.

The Cardinal tried to reassure her by reminding her that the Communist radio and newspapers had indulged in invectives against him for three years. He didn't succeed in calming her fears; she obviously felt that the Communists were preparing for a final showdown to get rid of him. At the end of the meal, she earnestly declared her support of the way her son was "defending the Church so heroically and conscientiously." On the other hand, she realized the danger that threatened him personally, and asked him if he couldn't do something to save his life by easing the tension between Church and State. We were both somewhat shaken by her anxious plea.

I remained with the Cardinal for a while and again brought up the question she had raised. I told him that various influential priests felt that the Cardinal should do whatever was necessary, short of abandoning his principles, in order to stay in office as long as possible. Here was the Cardinal's reply:

"This problem does not concern only the Catholic Church and Hungary, but the whole Christian world and Western civilization. ... Several times in history, we Hungarians have been in a strategic position where it was our mission to defend the Universal Church. Once when our nation was great and strong, we fulfilled our duty with the sword. Today we are no longer independent, but we still must courageously stand our ground in this struggle between Christianity and atheistic Bolshevism. Our historic mission is to alert and warn the rest of the world of the Communist threat. Our fulfillment of this task is far more important than winning a brief respite from our suffering at the price of a humiliating compromise."

Cardinal Mindszenty's Mother in 1948.

CHAPTER 7

No Rest in Mindszent

The next morning Cardinal Mindszenty said Mass at 7 A.M. in the parish church with his mother present to receive Communion from his hands. I said Mass for the parish, substituting for the pastor who had gone to visit the sick in neighboring Csipkerek. The boy who had been checking up on the secret police waited for me in the sacristy. He said he and his friends had kept watch all night, but found nothing unusual and the six strangers had left town after sunset.

The Cardinal read his breviary after Mass. After I finished my own Mass, we left for home. On the way, I told him of my suspicions and the boy's report. He showed surprise only at the way the secret police were now so conspicuous.

Mother Mindszenty had breakfast ready for us. We ate quickly, went over some documents, and at 10 o'clock started out on a long walk. Leaving the village on the highway to Mikospuszta, we walked down the path alongside the former Mesterházy estate.

The Cardinal led the conversation, reviving old childhood memories. I had the impression that he wanted to relive his experiences connected with his family and with this countryside before a witness who would be able to record them with credibility.(When I was his assistant pastor in Zalaegerszeg, we would walk together and he would frequently tell me about confidential clerical and personal affairs with the comment, "Someone else should have authentic knowledge of these matters.")

He recalled with gratitude his father who had worked hard as a farmer to finance his studies. The Cardinal spoke approvingly of his father's firmness in resisting any temptation to permit his family to share in any income of the church in Zalaegerszeg where his son was pastor. The church in Zalaegerszeg at that time needed many things which cost money, including a cultural center, another assistant pastor, and a girls' school. Substantial funds were always needed for the daily paper, repair of the rectory, and the home for the aged.

For a while, we discussed only specific religious and political problems. Then I brought up a new subject. In their constant calumny of the Cardinal, the Communists reproached him principally with refusing their peace offers and interfering with negotiations between Church and State. Since the Marxist press and radio had broadcast various derogatory innuendos, I bluntly asked him if anything were true in these accusations spread by the Communist propaganda apparatus. He replied that these accusations were "an orgy of hypocrisy," and then summed up the real situation.

Under Communist insistence, the Bishops' Conference agreed in February 1948 to send three delegates to meet representatives of the Government. The three delegates were Julius Czapik, Archbishop of Eger; László Bánáss, Bishop of Veszprém; and Coloman Papp, Bishop of Győr. They were authorized to negotiate a settlement between Church and State and to stipulate the Church's conditions for meaningful negotiations to begin.

The Government's delegation was headed by Communist Party boss Matthias Rákosi who kept stressing the urgent need for the Church to start negotiations with the new "democratic" State. The episcopal delegates presented the proposals of the Bishops' Conference: (1) the reestablishment of diplomatic relations with the Vatican; (2) permission for the publication of a daily newspaper which would articulate Christian ideology and culture; (3) permission for the disbanded Catholic associations to resume their activities; and (4) an end to the Communist Party's anti-religious propaganda issued through public agencies.

Rákosi listened to these conditions presented by the episcopal delegates and politely assured them that the Government in time would formally invite them to negotiate these issues. Actually, he did not consider them at all, and no invitation ever came. The Cardinal explained that the Communists didn't have the slightest intention of undoing the wrongs committed against the Church. Furthermore, their tactic of appearing to begin "negotiations" amounted to pressure for a "settlement" which would only further damage the Catholic Church.

The Cardinal wanted to visit the cemetery, so we turned off on a farm road leading toward the churchyard. We had hardly gone a hundred steps when we realized that we were being followed by some men in the cornfields about 15 to 20 yards away. Knowing that they could not be farmhands because it was the time they would all be at lunch, I suggested that we hurry. Without changing direction, we walked faster. Out of the corner of my eye, I recognized four of the young men who had watched our house the day before.

First we visited the grave of the Cardinal's father who had died in 1946 at the age of 82. It was well kept and decorated with flowers. Then we went to the graves of the Cardinal's three brothers who had died in childhood. The noon Angelus bell rang while we were there, so we said our prayers and hurried home for lunch.

Mother Mindszenty cooked and served us a delicious meal. In order to avoid another depressing conversation, the Cardinal questioned his mother about the coming harvest. She answered enthusiastically, happy that her two widowed daughters could anticipate sharing in a very good harvest. When she cleared the dishes, she said, "It wasn't such a bad lunch after all, was it?"

The Cardinal retorted, "You know very well that if you hadn't asked me I wouldn't have said anything!" The tenderness in his voice was his way of thanking her for an excellent meal.

After lunch, the Cardinal took a rest and I went to the rectory to take a nap. I hadn't slept more than 15 minutes when the pastor woke me, saying that a young stranger wanted to talk to the Cardinal. I went to the rectory door to see what he wanted. Rather arrogantly, he said he would speak only to the Cardinal whose life might depend on the news he was bringing.

I suggested that he give me the message because the Cardinal was resting, and rest was the reason he had come to Mindszent. The young man again said he had come in the Cardinal's interest, that his news concerned the Cardinal's life, and therefore he must see him personally. I told him he would have to wait at least an hour and even then there was no assurance he would be received. He chose to wait and sat on a bench in the rectory's garden while I said my breviary.

About an hour later, I went to tell the Cardinal about the strange visitor. The Cardinal was not inclined to see him. When I told the young man that His Eminence could not receive him, the young fellow started to talk. Speaking nervously, he told how that morning, in the police station at Vasvár where he was employed, he had overheard a telephone conversation between his district police chief and police headquarters in Szombathely. They were discussing the news that a sizable police force would arrive in Mindszent that evening because the Cardinal was in town.

This news did not surprise me as we had already seen some of the agents. I thanked the young man for his trouble and then returned to the Cardinal to report. He heard the news with equanimity, and we left for the vineyard to meet his mother at 4 P.M.

We walked the mile and a half between the village and the vineyard, over a meadow and along a dirt road. We had barely left the village when we heard a bicycle bell behind us. As the bicycler passed us, I noticed that he was the same young man who had brought the news from the police station. He recognized us, stopped some ten yards ahead of us and shouted back, "To be so close to the Primate of Hungary makes this the happiest day of my life." Then he rode off.

As we continued our walk, the same secret police agents appeared out of nowhere and played a sort of hide-and-seek in the cornfields. I asked the Cardinal if he didn't think we should return to Szombathely before sunset. He said, "Let's discuss that later and look for my mother first."

Mother Mindszenty, now 74 years old, had been working in the vineyard since noon. After her husband's death, she divided the property between her two daughters, keeping only three acres for herself. This was her only property and it was obviously carefully cultivated. She directed all the work herself, and personally did the lighter tasks from early spring to late fall. She cleaned and weeded the vines and fruit trees. The heavier work, including hoeing, cutting and spraying, was done by her grandchildren to whom she paid standard wages.

In the middle of the vineyard was the big three-room press-house. The center room contained the press and all the tools needed for the vineyard and fruit trees. The windowless cellar was delightfully cool and held an impressive array of barrels. Off the center room was a large, spacious room whose two windows gave a good view of the entire village. The furniture was simple but sturdy and comfortable. In the center of the room were a large table and chairs. A rustic old bench stood alongside one wall. On the opposite side were a couch and a stove. On the walls hung various pictures of patriotic scenes and national heroes. Among them was a picture of "Noah, the first vine grower," which the Cardinal's father had bought at a county fair. He was sentimental about this picture and liked to show it to guests, but Mother Mindszenty never cared for it.

At the west end of the property, on slightly higher ground, there was a low building with stalls, a shed, and some pigsties.

Mother Mindszenty greeted us in front of the press-house under the shade of a big tree. She was ready for us with a bottle of wine and dish of muffins. As we enjoyed her fine homemade vintage, the Cardinal asked about prospects for the fall harvest. "The vines are beautiful," she answered, "and we can hope for a good fruit harvest, too. I think we will be able to thank God for an exceptionally good year."

After our refreshments, we walked around the property whose every bush and flower she had planted and cared for.

Mother Mindszenty's press-house. This is where the grapes were pressed and where friends were served simple refreshments.

Mother Mindszenty working on her farm. This rare picture shows how she worked for her daily bread.

She proudly showed us her raspberries and red currant bushes, telling how she had fought destructive insects and cultivated her cherished plants. We left her at the small vegetable garden.

As the Cardinal and I walked toward the press-house, I again brought up the subject of our return. I suggested that both of us return by car to Szombathely, and that he stay there while I returned to Mindszent behind curtained windows so the secret police would not know that he was not with me. I could spend the night in his mother's house, and if I discovered anything suspicious I could report to him in the morning. Then he could decide whether to return to his mother's place, or go to Esztergom.

Before he had a chance to answer, we were surprised by the hurried arrival of the Rector of the Seminary, Monsignor Géfin. The Primate received him cordially and asked if he were the bearer of good news.

Monsignor Géfin replied: "I am sorry, but my news is rather serious. A courier from Budapest has just arrived with word that, at the urging of the Government, some of the Superiors of religious orders are negotiating with the State Minister of Education who has promised them they can keep some Catholic schools if the members of the religious orders will remain at their teaching positions in the expropriated schools. The Superiors are hoping that the Bishops' Conference will seriously consider this proposal."

Cardinal Mindszenty replied that the Bishops' Conference had already considered this and certainly would continue considering it if they thought such a move necessary under existing conditions. The nub of the problem was this: was it possible for members of religious orders to teach in atheistic Marxist schools and not be in daily conflict with their religious vows and Christian conscience? If the Government were to state officially that members of religious orders could teach according to conscience, then why was it necessary for the Government to take over the schools at all?

The Cardinal and the Rector would have discussed this problem at length if I had not pressed upon them the problem of whether we would be staying in Mindszent or leaving at

once for Szombathely. Monsignor Géfin immediately recommended our leaving and offered the Cardinal his own room
for the night. The Rector expressed a fear that the Communists might even kidnap the Cardinal during the night.
Such kidnappings were a typical Communist tactic as Monsignor Géfin, who had studied modern history extensively,
knew only too well. Of course, the Government would immediately declare it was "searching" for the victim and finally
conclude that there was "no trace."

The Cardinal finally agreed that it was better for him to
leave for Szombathely. He asked me to go tell his mother
that he had to leave after receiving some important news
from Esztergom.

When I reached Mother Mindszenty she had picked a
basketful of choice vegetables. I carried her basket and told
her the Rector from Szombathely had arrived with news
which required the Cardinal to leave immediately. Since it
was already rather late, she should not wait supper for us.
She sensed trouble right away.

After escorting her back to the press-house, I returned to
the village on foot. When I found our driver, I told him the
Cardinal had received some news from Esztergom which required us to go to Szombathely at once. The driver and I returned to the press-house and picked up the Cardinal. Mother
Mindszenty watched us leave with misty eyes but no other
sign of nervousness.

To throw the secret police off our trail, we took dirt roads
through the fields, avoiding the village altogether. The paths
through the woods were even worse. The car lurched and
shook as the driver tried to avoid the deep wheel tracks. We
were repeatedly bounced from our seats and several times
our heads banged against the top of the car. The Cardinal
remarked, "A Hungarian Primate has to be pretty hardy to
drive around here!"

We reached the highway some distance outside the village
and finally arrived at the Szombathely Seminary where the
Cardinal was welcomed into Monsignor Géfin's own room.
After supper I returned to Mindszent in the heavily-curtained
car and expected to be there by 11 P.M.

On the outskirts of Lipárt, we came up behind a harvesting machine which filled the narrow road so that we could not pass it. This meant that we had to drive very slowly in a constant cloud of dust. Our driver became quite nervous. He finally stopped, saying he would wait until the harvesting machine left the road, and then make up for lost time. After about ten minutes, when he tried to continue, our car wouldn't start. He pumped the gas pedal and pushed the starter again and again, but the engine would not turn over. He took the whole ignition system apart in vain. After an hour's tinkering with the engine, he finally found a point where the current had been interrupted. We then continued our trip without further difficulty, arriving in Mindszent just after midnight.

The Cardinal's mother was still awake. I had the task of telling her the Cardinal had to remain in Szombathely and we hoped to bring him back to Mindszent in the morning.

She gave me the guest room usually reserved for the Cardinal. I couldn't go to sleep right away and finally went to look out the window. Suddenly I heard steps and realized it was the young lad I had engaged to watch the secret police for me. "Did His Eminence arrive?" he whispered under the window. "How did you know he left?" I asked. "His mother told us he was leaving for Szombathely," he replied.

The boy then told me that about 20 secret police agents had reappeared in the village that evening, riding up and down the street. One of his friends had spotted a police van parked a few hundred yards from the homes on the highway. The riders had all come from this van. When they discovered that the Cardinal was no longer in the village, they returned to the van and drove off about 11 P.M.

In the morning when I told the Cardinal what had happened, he decided to return to Esztergom.

CHAPTER 8

The Third Arrest

The Communists continued their daily slanders against the Cardinal. They accelerated and "orchestrated" their attacks on the radio and through mass demonstrations. By autumn, posters and signs appeared with the slogan, "We must liquidate Mindszentyism!" Communist commentators reiterated emotional warnings that "peaceful coexistence between Church and State" depended on eliminating "Mindszentyism."

The Communists required the "progressive Catholics" to join in mass demonstrations against the Cardinal. School children and industrial workers were forced to listen to anti-Mindszenty harangues. The young people and workers were taught to repeat slogans and propaganda phrases demanding that the "obstinate" and "short-sighted" Cardinal be removed from his leadership of the Church so that "civil peace" could be restored.

This propaganda onslaught became so obnoxious that the Bishops' Conference, led by Archbishop Grösz, adopted this public protest at a special meeting on November 3, 1948:

"The Conference of Bishops expresses its dismay and consternation at the unjust and shameful attacks systematically launched against Cardinal Mindszenty on the radio and in public meetings. In the name of religious liberty, the Bishops' Conference raises its voice against such attacks. The Hungarian Bishops assure the Cardinal of their complete confidence in him and loyalty to him; they unite and identify themselves with him in his struggle to defend the best interests of the Church, the people, and the Hungarian nation."[1]

To "liquidate the Mindszenty problem," the Communists then mobilized their so-called "democratic forces," just as they had done when they expropriated the schools. Communist agents appeared in offices and factories, and even in many private homes, to "enlighten" the citizens about the

Cardinal's "anti-democratic" attitude and to summon every-one to join in the fight against "Mindszentyism." They inti-midated a few people into signing statements calling for his punishment and removal. The National Committee of Com-munes, which was entirely controlled by the Communists, was ordered to present petitions to the Parliament demand-ing the arrest and trial of the Cardinal.

In an address to the nation on November 18, 1948 the Cardinal responded to this demand for his illegal arrest: "In spite of repeated promises made since World War II, no elections have been held anywhere except in the capital. Thus, there is no legal basis for any governmental actions in the cities, counties or districts. Men are forced to make declara-tions contrary to general public opinion by being threatened with the loss of their bread or freedom.

"The majority has been silenced and excluded from the exercise of their constitutional rights. 'Freedom of speech' in this new 'democracy' does not permit any criticism. If any is voiced, then the critic is fired from his job! This has happened time and time again. All my sympathy goes out to those who oppose this regime. Their sterling examples of character, loyalty, and courage are inspiring."[2]

From every stratum of society all over Hungary, an im-pressive number of letters and delegations arrived in Esz-tergom to assure the Cardinal of their continuing concern, loyalty, and gratitude. On November 18, he also issued this message to reassure those worried about his life:

"I calmly watch the storm artificially blown about my person. In my position, storms are not uncommon. History provides many examples. Two of my predecessors died in battles. Two had all their possessions confiscated. John Vitéz was thrown in prison. Martinuzzi was assassinated by hired killers. Pázmány, one of the greatest, was exiled. Ambrus Károly became the victim of an epidemic as he visited the sick.

"None of my 48 predecessors, however, was the victim of so many deliberate trumped-up lies, obstinately repeated even though they have been refuted a hundred times.

"I stand firmly for God, Church, and Country in my his-

toric responsibility to the nation which has repeatedly stood
alone against the enemies of Western civilization. Compared
to the sufferings of my people, my own fate is not important."

Cardinal Mindszenty ended this message with these words:
"Only reluctantly do I reply to my accusers. The anguish of
my people, their tears and the injustices they endure, oblige
me to speak out and state the facts. I pray for a world of
justice and charity. I pray also for those who, as the Master
has said, know not what they do. I forgive them from my
heart."[3]

The next day, November 19, 1948, Father Andrew Zakar,
the Cardinal's personal secretary, was arrested. He was simply
kidnapped on the street about 7:00 A.M. as he was returning
from Mass to his lodging in the Archbishop's residence. Three
days later, the secret police searched his entire apartment as
well as some other rooms in the residence.

Cardinal Mindszenty released a public statement in
which he exonerated from guilt any Catholic man or woman
who was forced to sign a declaration against him, "since he
or she does not act deliberately." He said that he did not
want "any individuals or families to suffer or lose their jobs"
on his account.[4]

Still continuing the propaganda attack, the Communist
radio and press published letters signed by some "progressive
Catholics" as well as by a few prominent Catholics who had
been intimidated into adding their names. Cardinal Mindszenty issued the following reply:

"These letters allege that I have hurt the Church in Hungary and caused its problems, and they urge a change in my
position and behavior. . . . I ask these writers, however, to
look at the facts. The same Church-State relationship exists
at the present time in other Eastern European countries.
These letters echo the optimistic line of the Hungarian press
that the Church leaders in Czechoslovakia, Yugoslavia, Rumania, Bulgaria and Poland have recently developed a
'democratic' attitude.

"These letters state that one Archbishop is an avowed
partisan of his Communist regime; another celebrated a *Te
Deum* at the installation of the Communist Republic's leaders;

another led his bishops in procession to swear allegiance to the Communist 'democratic' state. All these examples are intended to reflect unfavorably on the Church in Hungary.

"With such a 'cordial' relationship, there ought to be a flourishing religious life in those countries. But look! Even the Communist press has to admit that Archbishop Beran and Cardinal Sapieha are 'not cooperating.' In Rumania, four Bishops at one time were arrested. These letter writers forget that what we have in Hungary is materialistic and atheistic Communism — and its anti-religious attitude is not caused by me or by the Church."[5]

The Archbishop's residence in Esztergom was searched again on December 23, 1948. The secret police brought with them Father Andrew Zakar whom they had "treated" and brainwashed for a month. Father Zakar was in a pathetic, dazed condition. He walked with strange dancing steps up and down the corridors and babbled incessantly that he had been among kind people who had even given him "bits of meat." His incredible conduct terrified everyone who lived in the Archbishop's residence. The secret police then took Father Zakar into the cellar, emerging triumphantly with a large tin tube which they said contained documents revealing a conspiracy against the Government.

The documents "found" in the tin tube were immediately shown to the press which trumpeted the news that these "documents of the Cardinal's conspiracy" would be used by the prosecution at the trial. The fact was that these documents had been collected by the Communists beforehand. They were letters written by Cardinal Mindszenty to various Western prelates urging that the famous Crown of St. Stephen, the most sacred treasure of Christian Hungary, be transferred from the United States to the Vatican. The courier who carried the letters had unfortunately fallen into the hands of the

Esztergom Cathedral and the Primate's Residence where Cardinal Mindszenty was arrested on December 26, 1948.

Communists and could save his life only by handing over the entire correspondence to the secret police.[6]

The search of the residence was deliberately conducted so that the Cardinal would meet his secretary and see what a physical and mental wreck he was from brainwashing and drugs. The purpose of the secret police was, of course, to frighten the Cardinal. They made sure he got the message that he, too, would have his mind and will destroyed if he fell into their hands.

Even this diabolical threat could not frighten the Cardinal or induce him to save his own skin by repudiating the rights of the Church or by fleeing the country. That same night, he showed his courage in the face of this threat by writing the following declaration which exposed in advance the crooked methods of Soviet trials:

"I never participated in any kind of conspiracy. I will not resign my office as Archbishop. I have nothing to confess and I won't sign anything. If you should ever read that I have confessed or resigned, and even see it authenticated by my signature, remember that it will have been only the result of human frailty. In advance, I declare all such actions null and void."

He put the paper into an envelope, sealed it and wrote on it instructions that, after his arrest, it should be given to the Archbishop Joseph Grősz, the vice chairman of the Bishops' Conference.

After the second search of the Archbishop's residence, two of his other priests were arrested: Father Emery Bóka, the Archdiocesan accountant, and Father John Fábián, the Cardinal's second secretary. They joined Father Zakar at 60 Andrássy Street, the Budapest prison headquarters of the secret police.

The Cardinal's mother had arrived at Esztergom shortly before the second searching of the residence. The Cardinal showed his continuing affection for his mother by inviting her to his official residence for the important feasts and to attend the ceremonies at the Cathedral. This time she had come to spend the Christmas season.

After the search of the residence, which naturally upset

everyone in the household, the Cardinal and his mother, together with the only remaining priest in the Chancery, ate a simple supper. When they finished, the Cardinal took his mother to her room on the first floor and stayed with her in private conversation for a rather long time. She told me about this conversation when I saw her later in her home in Mindszent during the interval between the Cardinal's arrest and trial.

She was much upset by the house search, but even more by Father Zakar's strange behavior. Disturbed by his condition, she urged her son to leave immediately for Rome in order to save his own life. She told him that she had received numerous letters from friends who were worried about his life, and they all pinned their hope for his safety on a flight to Rome. She told me that her pleading obviously distressed the Cardinal, who replied that he would not desert either his country or his people in such troubled times. "A pastor of souls must stay with his flock," he said, "and cannot flee like a hired servant." Continuing he told her:

"I know very well what my arrest and perhaps execution by the Communists would mean to you at your age of 74. I know this would break your heart. I have known for a long time, Mother, that great grief would be your lot. But please take comfort from the Blessed Mother whose heart was also pierced under the Cross by the arrows of pain. For a long time I have prayed to the Sorrowful Mother to give you the grace to accept God's will about my suffering and death."

Mother Mindszenty told me she was encouraged by her son's spirit of martyrdom and patriotism. He gave her the strength to endure his arrest and the agonizing suspense of the weeks preceding his trial. "With God's help, I was able to make you happy for a while. Now, you must take up your cross," he said in parting.

It is clear that Cardinal Mindszenty made a conscious decision to stay at his post in Hungary when he could so easily have escaped to Rome. He knew that the torture and murder of other priests at 60 Andrássy Street simply had made no significant impact on the Western world. He felt that it was his responsibility to stay and confront the Com-

munists in order that the Free World would learn how even
the strongest man can be broken and debased by the diabolical tortures of the Bolshevik bosses.

From December 16 on, the Archbishop's home had been
constantly surrounded by the secret police. That was the
last meeting of the Bishops' Conference under Cardinal
Mindszenty's chairmanship. It was obvious that the Communist regime had mobilized the secret police in order to terror-
ize the Bishops and lay the groundwork for the Cardinal's
arrest. Secret police screened every visitor, and only those on
official business could enter the offices or see the Cardinal.

On December 26, 1948 an armed squad of the secret
police broke into the Archbishop's residence in Esztergom and
arrested Cardinal Mindszenty. His mother watched and bade
him a tearful goodbye. Taking only a small handbag and
his breviary, he climbed into the van, and the vile-talking
police drove him to their dreaded headquarters at 60 Andrássy Street. He was completely calm and composed. This
was the third time in his life that he had been subjected to
the traumatic experience of an arrest.

Western radios broadcast the news, together with portions
of the Cardinal's pastoral letter to his priests dated December
21. These excerpts show the spiritual quality of his leadership
in a time of crisis:

"Everywhere and always, only that happens which God
permits. Without His knowledge, not a single hair falls from
our heads. The world can deprive us of many things, but it
cannot take away our faith in Jesus Christ. Who can separate
us from Him? Neither death nor life nor any other creature
can separate us from the love of God, which is in Christ Jesus
our Lord. *(Romans 8:38-39)*. What he has told us is valid
for all times. Do not worry about your life, or what you shall
eat, or what you shall wear; your Heavenly Father will care
for you. We cannot behave like men without faith or hope.

"Let us pray for those among us whose nerves are frayed by present events, and who alarm and panic others around them. Let us pray that the bell of peace will toll in their tormented hearts, and that their way will be lighted by the Lord's question to His disciples on the stormy sea, 'Why are you fearful, O ye of little faith?'

"Let us pray that the lesson of St. John Chrysostom may bring peace to our troubled hearts. Although he was plagued by persecution and heavy crosses, nevertheless peace filled his heart and he addressed his faithful from the harbor of Constantinople with these words: 'The waves roar and the storm rages, but we are not afraid because the rock of the Church cannot be crushed. Despite the hurricane around us, the Lord's ship cannot sink. After all, what is there to fear? Death? My life is Christ and death would be my gain. Exile? The Lord has given us the whole world and its beauty. Confiscation? We did not bring anything into this world, and we can take nothing out of it. I despise that with which the world tries to frighten me. I laugh at the way the world tries to seduce me. I urge you to remain indomitably courageous and unfalteringly firm.'

"Therefore, my friends, don't worry about tomorrow. Let us find our consolation in the Gospels and in the history of the world and our nation. Our Christian and Hungarian ancestors have never enjoyed soft lives. St. Paul, the apostle of suffering and persecution, sends us this message: 'For whatsoever things were written aforetime were written for our learning, that we through patience and comfort of the Scriptures might have hope.' (Romans 15:4) . . .

"Priests, religious and nuns are expected to give an example of standing firm at their posts. Our profession of faith must be a beacon to the faithful, to the members of other denominations, and to atheists. They must know more surely than ever before that 'We are made a spectacle unto the world, and to angels, and to men.' (1 Corinthians 4:9).

"Let us be a light shining in the darkness. According to our own abilities, let us each work with all our might to win the kingdom of God which is the world of justice and grace. On our way to God, we cannot forget the words of Tertullian:

'The accusations of our accusers are our glory.' Everything we have done has been to preserve the liberty of the Church, to safeguard our youth, to help our own suffering people, for peace, for higher spiritual values – and not for the reasons they accuse us. . . .

"By the grace of God, we can rise to the heights of the Apostles who were willing to suffer flogging and ignominy for the love of Christ. Ours is the world of the Sermon on the Mount. 'Blessed are those who suffer persecution for justice' sake, for theirs is the kingdom of Heaven. Blessed are you when men shall revile you and persecute you, and shall say all manner of evil against you falsely, for my sake.' *(Matthew 5:10-11)* . . .

"The hope of eternal life promised by the Lord shall brighten our eyes. 'Be of good cheer; I have overcome the world.' *(John 16:33)*."[7]

The Cardinal's mother spent the whole night in prayer in the guest room of the Archbishop's residence. The next day she went to Budapest to begin her long struggle to save her son's life from the cruelty of the Communists.

CHAPTER 9

The Mock Trial

Mother Mindszenty accepted the hospitality of a Convent in Budapest and the assistance of one of the nuns, Sister Elizabeth, who later wrote a newspaper article summing up her experiences:[1]

"Shortly after the Cardinal's arrest, his 74-year-old mother arrived in Budapest. I was sent to meet her at the train station and to welcome her to our Convent. I assisted her during her stay and accompanied her from bureau to bureau as she sought permission to visit her son.

"She met several times with a relative who was a Supreme Court Judge. He helped her retain a defense attorney, Dr. Andrew Farkas. This courageous lawyer was willing to defend the Cardinal and made several unsuccessful attempts to see him in the prison at 60 Andrássy Street. Both the Judge and the lawyer advised us not to abandon our entreaties on Andrássy Street or at the Ministry of the Interior until we won recognition of the Cardinal's right to see counsel during his pre-trial detention.

"We were not surprised that our requests were rejected at both places. The Communist officials flatly refused permission for the Cardinal's mother to see him. Finally, one day they seemed more inclined to listen to us. They tried to calm the Cardinal's mother by smilingly telling her that her son already had a defense lawyer named Coloman Kiczkó, and that the Cardinal had personally written to Kiczkó asking him to serve.

"When we told this to our two legal advisers, they were shocked because they knew Kiczkó was an oldtime Communist who had played an important role in the 1919 Communist dictatorship. This opened our eyes to the fact that the Government was preparing a trial which would be a travesty of justice. This convinced both Dr. Farkas and the

104

Supreme Court Judge that nothing could be done to help the Primate. Torn by an increasing fear that the Communists were preparing to execute her son, the Cardinal's mother returned to Mindszent."

Hearing that Mother Mindszenty had returned home, I went to see her. She told me of her frustrating efforts in Budapest and that the "defense counsel," Coloman Kiczkó, had called on her. Kiczkó showed her his letter of credentials, handwritten by the Cardinal. Kiczkó said several times that the case would be tried by an independent court and that he, as defense counsel, would do everything he could to aid his client. She asked Kiczkó to contact Dr. Farkas who was willing to cooperate in every way, but Kiczkó absolutely refused to do this. Of course, she did not believe his lies.

I tried to allay Mother Mindszenty's fears that the Communists would kill her son. I cited the volume of protests expressed throughout the entire Free World and the indignation shown by the Western press. I argued that the Communists would only hurt themselves by his execution. Such a miscarriage of justice would awaken public opinion in the Free World to the basic inhumanity of Communism. She replied, "God grant that the world will recognize the danger of Communism."

Soon after my visit with Mother Mindszenty, the Government published the so-called *Yellow Book*, officially titled *Documents on the Mindszenty Case*.[2] Among the documents included was a "confession of general political views" handwritten in Hungarian with numerous misspellings and errors. Here is the text of Cardinal Mindszenty's alleged "confession":

"I am a Hungarian nobleman. My original surname was Pehm. The Pehm family was declared noble in 1732. On my maternal side, I am descended from the Hungarian noble family called Kovács, which was elevated to the nobility in 1663. I was sent to Zalaegerszeg as a Catholic religion teacher in February 1917. I was assigned there as pastor in 1919. In this capacity, I worked there until March 29, 1944, when I became Bishop of Veszprém.

"Looking back on my public life, I declare that I always

considered myself a royalist. Therefore, I enthusiastically supported whatever political movements would help realize this objective.

"After my appointment as Primate, I could work for these objectives more effectively. My aim is identical with the goal of the Hungarian royalist movement: a Federal Central European Monarchy formed by a union of Hungary and Austria, possibly joining with other Catholic states such as Bavaria, with Otto von Hapsburg as our King. I thought this objective would be possible only after the overthrow of the Hungarian Republic and with help from abroad, especially from America.

"Therefore, on the one hand, I did everything possible to obtain American help for Hungary. On the other hand, I worked against the Hungarian Republic by urging American intervention through espionage and supplying information on a regular basis.

"To achieve my objective, I not only relied on the Americans, but I tried to unite all the forces in Hungary and abroad who were working to overthrow the Republic, and who wanted to conceal the Republic's successes such as agricultural reform and the nationalization of the schools.

"I expected the restoration of the monarchy after an American victory in a Third World War. During the period of transition and until the establishment of the House of Hapsburg, I would have been temporary Head of State. I wanted to crown Otto because he would have assured me every privilege characteristic of the First Peer of the realm.

"I acknowledge that, since my youth, I have stood against every democratic movement of the Hungarian people, and have always supported rightist movements.

"Joseph Mindszenty"

My colleagues and I, all professors at the Theological Seminary, examined the *Yellow Book's* handwritten "confession," suspecting that it was a forgery. Our suspicion was confirmed not only by the "confession's" obvious falsehoods (even the date of his consecration as Bishop was wrong), but by its primitive misspellings and misplaced words. The "confession" contained 50 misspellings, including 28 rather flagrant ones. The title "Primate" was misspelled; the word "Catholic" was written with two different misspellings; even such words as "Monarchy" and "Peer" were misspelled. About 20 words which naturally belonged together were separated. The accent marks were generally wrong. Letters were omitted from many words.

Based on such misspellings, we feared that this "confession" might not be a simple forgery, i.e., a complete fabrication, as were many of the documents in the *Yellow Book,* because we thought that forgers would not dare to produce such an illiterate document allegedly written by a Cardinal. We came to the chilling conclusion that the Cardinal might have written it himself while in a half-conscious state after being completely brainwashed and drugged. If this were true, we thought the Communists would have to execute the Cardinal after the trial in order to prevent their vicious cruelty from becoming public knowledge.

After reading the *Yellow Book,* I was so worried that I went to see a leading physician who was the head of a hospital, to get more information about brainwashing effects. I asked him if he had read the alleged "confession" of Cardinal Mindszenty.

"Yes, I read it several times," he answered.

"What is your opinion? Have they completely destroyed the Cardinal's mind?"

"I don't think so. This could happen if he were deprived of rest and sleep for days at a time. If someone is completely exhausted like this, one or two morphine shots can induce a trance-like state of somnambulism under which a 'confession' could be obtained."

The press and radio belabored the contents of the *Yellow Book* until its falsehoods were known to everyone. Mother Mindszenty's local pastor telephoned me to say that she was completely unstrung by the false "confession." He asked me to come and comfort her.

When I went to visit her, she immediately brought up the subject of the *Yellow Book* and the "confession", saying: "You see, the Communists are not afraid of anything. They have already destroyed his mind, and after the trial they will kill him."

I tried to comfort her, saying: "I am still convinced that they do not dare to condemn the Cardinal to death, much less to execute him. I think they devised the *Yellow Book* to blackmail the Vatican and the Bishops' Conference into negotiations. Instead of a phony trial which would cause a world scandal, they published the *Yellow Book* to put pressure on the Bishops' Conference."

"The whole thing is terrifying," she replied. "How could they force my son to write such lies — and with such bad spelling?"

I recounted my conversation with the doctor at the hospital, stressing again that the Cardinal would recover and that the Communists would not dare execute him.

When I saw the Cardinal years later in Budapest on November 1, 1956, after his liberation by the Hungarian Freedom Fighters, he personally told me about his pre-trial detention and how he had been subjected to day-and-night interrogation, hour after hour without any sleep, by brutal interrogators working in shifts. He was forced to stand with arms raised high for days at a time under blinding lights, during endless repetition of rapid-fire questions. Despite extreme physical and psychological tortures, for the first 15 days he did not make any kind of confession and did not sign anything.

Thus, there was no truth whatsoever to the announcement by the Ministry of the Interior on December 29, 1948, the third day after his arrest, that: "Confronted by massive evidence, Joseph Mindszenty, Archbishop of Esztergom, has pleaded guilty."

The Cardinal signed a "confession" on January 11 when he felt on the verge of a complete breakdown and hoped to get rid of his interrogators at least for a few hours. Under his signature, he placed the letters "c.f." for *"coactus feci"*,

Cardinal Mindszenty with his Communist lawyer, Coloman Kiczkó. This picture was taken at a recess during the mock trial. Note the avid listener behind them.

that is, "I signed under force." The interrogators took the "confession" triumphantly, but soon returned after secret police experts deciphered the meaning of the Latin letters.

The relentless interrogation was immediately resumed. When he was physically broken by three weeks of grueling day-and-night interrogation, tormented with pain, and unable to say "no" any longer, the "treatment" with drugs began.[3] On January 19, the secret police published the *Yellow Book* containing the alleged "confession." It was a complete forgery — obviously hurriedly prepared by uneducated interrogators — and the Cardinal never wrote or signed any confession at all.

Prior to Cardinal Mindszenty's arrest, the secret police had successfully used their inhuman techniques to induce many other "confessions." But no other victim had ever defied his tormentors for so long a period.

Even the "confession," however, did not end Cardinal Mindszenty's "pre-trial processing" by the secret police. The "treatment" with drugs and interrogation continued in order to convince him that he was really guilty of crimes and to turn him into a witness against himself. Only this "treatment" could have persuaded him to accept the Communist Kiczkó as his defense lawyer. Cardinal Mindszenty was subjected to 40 days of "processing" by brainwashing and drugs at the hands of the secret police in the Budapest prison at 60 Andrássy Street.

In typical Communist procedure, no one was permitted to see him during this period except his interrogators and those who were preparing his trial. Not even his mother or Dr. Farkas, whom she wanted as defense counsel, was allowed to visit him.

When Cardinal Mindszenty's public trial finally opened on February 3, 1949 the effects of the drugs and Communist-style brainwashing were obvious to everyone. He looked like a man broken physically and mentally. We had known Cardinal Mindszenty as a man of vigor and independence; at the trial, he appeared awkward, submissive, slavishly obedient to every directive of the court. He "confessed" against himself in a long stream of self-accusations. If he forgot memorized lines and momentarily stumbled in reciting them, the court was always quick to help him continue the prewritten dialogue.

It was a pathetic sight. Spectators could not help but sympathize when Cardinal Mindszenty and the other prisoners on trial pleaded guilty and recited their nearly-identical memorized "confessions" in weary, impassive tones.[4] His behavior at the trial was so out of character that a rumor circulated in Budapest that the Cardinal was dead and an actor had played his part at the trial.

The trial of Cardinal Mindszenty, February 3 to 8, 1949, was one of the dramatic events of our era. The Communist-appointed "defense counsel", Coloman Kiczkó, seemed to realize this when he said that it "will be remembered in world history." At the end of this mock trial, Cardinal Mindszenty was convicted of treason, trying to overthrow the Government, and foreign currency speculation, and he was condemned to life imprisonment.

Even though drugs, sleeplessness, and 40 days of psychological and physical pounding had manipulated the Cardinal into playing a self-accusatory role at the trial, and even though the Government carefully controlled the news accounts of the trial, nevertheless the Free World got the message that Communist diabolical techniques had made a mockery of justice. Shortly after the trial, a crowd of more than 100,000 gathered in St. Peter's Square in Rome to protest. Pope Pius XII told them:

"The physical condition of Cardinal Mindszenty can only be explained by secret and unknown influences. This man, by nature so extremely vigorous, was suddenly changed into a frail and broken character — so much so that his behavior is an accusation not against the accused, but against the accusers."[5]

In America, newspapers, public officials and churchmen of all faiths denounced the trial in the strongest language. In New York City, 4,000 Boy Scouts marched under the banner "Pray for Cardinal Mindszenty." On February 9, 1949, the U.S. House of Representatives unanimously passed a resolution expressing the shock of the civilized world and

Pope Pius XII receiving diplomats at the Vatican. These are some of the various diplomats who on February 10, 1949 called on the Pope to express their sympathy for Cardinal Mindszenty who had been condemned to life imprisonment.

Cardinal Mindszenty at the mock trial. Standing on the right is Father Justin Baranyay, a Cistercian and university professor who was condemned to 15 years in prison.

urging "that these issues shall be raised by the United States, either in the United Nations or by such other means as may be most appropriate."

My original suspicion that the *Yellow Book* was designed to pressure and intimidate the Bishops was confirmed. The Communists hoped to force them into negotiations with the Government during the Cardinal's captivity. In the last week of January, Archbishop Grősz even received a "letter from Cardinal Mindszenty" asking the Bishops to begin negotiations with the Government. The letter recommended, as a first step, that the Bishops attend the reception given by the Hungarian President on February 1, the anniversary of the Communist Republic.

Even though this letter appeared to be the Cardinal's own handwriting, the majority of Bishops indignantly rejected it as a fraud. Archbishop Grősz, who had succeeded as chairman of the Bishops' Conference after the Cardinal's arrest, forbade any Bishop to appear at the reception. Four of the 16 members of the Conference attended anyway: Julius Czapik, Archbishop of Eger, John Drahos, Vicar General of Esztergom, and Bishops Nicholas Dudás and Andrew Hamvas.

The next day the newspapers, in typical Communist fashion, falsely reported that Archbishop Czapik had said at the reception: "The Bishops' Conference entrusts the decision of what to do with Cardinal Mindszenty to the wise judgment of the Government."[6]

Nevertheless, due to the strong resistance of Pope Pius XII, Archbishop Grősz, and the majority of Hungarian Bishops, the Government failed completely in its attempt to force the Hungarian Church into "negotiations" on Communist terms.

In the wake of the mock trial's flagrant violation of human dignity, the Communist manipulators of the crooked trial had to do something to appease world indignation. They sent Cardinal Mindszenty to the hospital in the Central Prison in Budapest for two full weeks in order to erase the effects of the mind-paralyzing drugs which had so debilitated him for his public ordeal. As soon as they felt it was safe to do so, they showed the Cardinal to his mother and to his Vicar in Budapest, Dr. Béla Witz.

Sister Elizabeth's newspaper article contains a good description of Mother Mindszenty's first visit to her son in prison after his conviction:

"Cardinal Mindszenty's mother returned to Budapest after the verdict. She was extremely worried, but tried to hope that her son would not be executed. She only wanted to see him as soon as possible and talk with him, since she was afraid that he might have been deprived of the use of his mind and will, and might never again be a sane man.

"She resumed her entreaties to see the Cardinal. She started at the place where the public trial was held on Markó Street, but was simply told that he was no longer there. At the headquarters of the secret police on Andrássy Street and at the Ministry of Justice, we were told they did not know where he was. They would not even answer our question as to who had authority to grant permission to see him. Two weeks had passed since the end of the trial when finally, on February 23, the Under Secretary in the Ministry of Justice, Stephen Timár, told us that only Gabriel Péter, the head of the secret police, knew the Cardinal's whereabouts and could grant permission for visitors.

"We naturally went immediately to see Gabriel Péter. We had to wait a long time in the lobby. Finally a female secretary asked what we wanted. Péter then received us and asked who had told us to come to him. We told him the Ministry of Justice. He remarked that they were wrong in presuming that he could grant permission for a visit.

"He then turned to the Cardinal's mother and arrogantly said, 'Do you know that I could have searched your house upside down since your traitor-son confessed he had sent documents there for safekeeping?'

" 'That is true,' she answered quietly. 'He sent me a package containing all the letters I had written him since he was a young student.'

" 'You see! That proves that in this country no secret can be kept from our democratic police!'

"With great dignity she replied, 'I don't see what kind of secrets you could hope to find in a mother's letters.'

"Then she begged Péter to grant her permission to visit her son. He again refused, saying he did not have the authority. Then I began to plead. I spoke with great feeling about this simple request of a grief-stricken old woman. How could he not be affected by the anguish of an elderly mother, heart-broken by uncertainty over her son's fate? All she wanted in life was to see her son. I asked him to think how his own mother might feel in such a situation. I begged him to be merciful and not refuse her this small consolation.

"Péter then promised he would phone someone and try to arrange a visit. He disappeared into another room for a few moments, and then returned, saying: 'It is all settled. You can see your son. You can spend 15 minutes with him. But weigh carefully any words you speak to him — or this visit will be your last. The only topics of conversation can be family matters. You will go in a police car accompanied by persons I will appoint.'

"We waited in the lobby for the escort, which finally arrived: two members of the secret police, a man and a woman. The Cardinal's mother asked them to take her to her lodgings first so she could pick up a parcel. Péter, who overheard this, said there was no time for any delay as they were expected immediately at the prison.

"The policewoman asked the Cardinal's mother what it was that she wanted to take her son. She answered, 'A few apples and some cake.' Péter took out his wallet and handed some money to the policewoman to buy four pounds of apples in a nearby shop to take to the Cardinal.

"Of course, I could not accompany them. I later learned that, when they arrived at the prison, the guards were ready for them. The gate was opened immediately and the driver took them directly to the prison hospital. The Cardinal's mother went inside, accompanied by the policeman, and sat down in a shabby reception room.

"Almost at once, Cardinal Mindszenty walked in. He rushed to embrace her, saying, 'Mother, you found me even here! How did you ever find me?'

"After she returned to my Convent, she told me the details of her brief visit. 'My son was very happy to see me and wanted to know how I was. We talked some minutes about the family; he was interested in each one. I gave him the apples, but did not tell him that Gabriel Péter had paid for them!'

"I asked her, 'Did you notice anything different about the Cardinal's mind indicating that he might have undergone a change while in prison?' Her voice thrilled with the answer: 'He is absolutely the same. He remembered everybody and everything. Thank God my son is healthy in mind and body. I can't tell you how happy I am to find him alive and well!'"

CHAPTER 10

The Cardinal Disappears

There were indications that the Communists had miscalculated in choosing their timing for Cardinal Mindszenty's arrest.

The so-called "progressive Catholics" in Hungary had been negotiating with the Communists for a solution of the "Mindszenty problem." As a result of this "dialogue," the "progressive Catholics" had been won over to the view that the Catholic Church in Hungary could live in "peaceful coexistence" under the present Government only if Cardinal Mindszenty were removed from his key position as Primate. By December 1948, when it became evident that the Communists wanted to get rid of him at any price, the "progressive Catholics" considered the time ripe for asking the Vatican to arrange such a "solution." They were convinced that the six-month campaign of slander had adequately prepared world opinion, including the Vatican, for the Cardinal's arrest.

These "progressive Catholics" had already engaged in various stratagems against Cardinal Mindszenty — but he had astutely evaded their cunning intrigues and they had been able to produce only meager results for their Bolshevik bosses. Now these "progressive Catholics" hoped to persuade Vatican officials that the problems between the Church and the Hungarian Government were caused by the Cardinal's "obstinate" behavior.

Proceeding on this assumption, in December 1948 the "progressives" offered their services to the Government to try to solve the "Mindszenty problem" by making an overture to the Holy See. They assumed that, in the current strained situation, the Vatican would feel obliged to remove the Cardinal from his position as Hungarian Primate. As their messenger, the "progressives" sent a Hungarian Jesuit who arrived in Rome at Christmas, 1948.

118

He had hardly rested up from his long trip when he heard the news that the Communist Government had arrested Cardinal Mindszenty on December 26. Left out on a limb, the "progressive" Jesuit was heard to remark, "How could they commit such a stupidity at the very moment of my arrival in Rome!"

There is no doubt that the Communists had for some time intended to exclude the Cardinal from all Church-State negotiations. In falsely announcing the Cardinal's "confession" on December 29, the Minister of the Interior added that his own "investigations" showed that Cardinal Mindszenty had organized a "conspiracy" against the Government, spied for foreign powers, and smuggled foreign currency.[1] The Communists expected the Cardinal's "confession" to be their trump card in forcing the Vatican to negotiate on Communist terms.

Vatican officials, however, saw through such obvious Communist tactics, and Pope Pius XII decreed that the Hungarian "progressives" could not negotiate about Cardinal Mindszenty, but *only* about the Vatican regulation of January 2, 1949 which forbade the Hungarian Bishops to negotiate with the Communist Government. *L'Osservatore Romano*, the Vatican's semi-official newspaper, published the following declaration on January 4, 1949:

"The Vatican has informed the Hungarian Government that, without prejudice to Cardinal Mindszenty, it reserves to itself the right to make any agreement between the Catholic Church and the Hungarian Government.

"The Vatican replied to the Hungarian Government as follows:

"1. It is incomprehensible how the alleged desire for an agreement with the Vatican can be reconciled with the mistreatment given an Archbishop, Primate and Cardinal — mistreatment which is very offensive to the Holy See.

"2. The Vatican position remains that the rights of the Church and the right to freedom of conscience must be respected. This means not only freedom of worship, but freedom to give religious instruction, freedom to preach the

Gospel and propagate the faith, and especially freedom to give children a Christian education."[2]

Other slanders hurled against Cardinal Mindszenty included the charge that his arrest was precipitated by his espousing religious and political views contrary to those of the Pope. Pius XII himself replied:

"The uncalled-for arrest of our beloved son, Joseph Cardinal Mindszenty, Archbishop of Esztergom, and his removal from his episcopal seat, has grieved us most deeply. Such a lack of reverence and respect toward this highly esteemed Prince of the Church is a deep offense to religion and human dignity.

"Therefore, conscience and duty compel us to openly express our sorrow and grief for these violations of the rights of the Church. We voice an indignation and concern felt not only by Hungarian Catholics, but by Catholics everywhere. We solemnly protest this injustice inflicted on the whole Catholic Church.

"The great merits of this Prince of the Church, as well as his unshakable faith, are well known to us. We know also his apostolic courage and firmness in protecting Christian doctrine and the sacred rights of the Church. He should not be blamed, but praised, for the accusations and slanders uttered against him. As Archbishop, he fulfilled his unflinching duty to watch over the Church with a courageous and steadfast heart, despite the way the liberty of the Church has been curtailed and handicapped in every way, especially the way Christian doctrine has been prevented from being taught, and the faithful prevented from attending religious services. He rightly insisted that freedom of religion could not be limited to church services alone, but must include the schools, the press, pilgrimages to sacred shrines, and the activities of Catholic organizations."[3]

The Hungarian Bishops' Conference ceased their preparations for negotiations with the Communists, informing the Government that they could not attend the meeting scheduled for January 8. The Bishops informed the laity of their decision in a short pastoral letter, stating: "In negotiations with the Government on Church-State relations, canon law obliges us to act in harmony with the Holy See, rather than deciding such questions by ourselves."[4]

Having failed in their efforts to trick either the Hungarian Bishops or the Vatican into negotiations on Communist terms, the Government proceeded with its shameful mock trial described in the preceding chapter.

The shocking violation of human rights exposed so glaringly in Cardinal Mindszenty's mock trial made a stunning impression on the entire civilized world. Millions of people everywhere were spellbound by the dramatic events in Budapest which showed that the Communists — by the use of drugs and devilish torture — had changed a naturally courageous and uncompromising opponent into a broken shadow of his former self. Throughout the world, there were mass protests by various religious and social organizations. Parliamentary leaders and heads of state, as well as leaders of every religious faith, vigorously protested this outrage against justice. In Hungary, which was more than two-thirds Catholic, the Calvinist, Lutheran, Jewish and other faiths were keenly aware that *their* religious freedom depended on whatever religious freedom the Catholics were able to maintain.

Added to the horror at such spectacular injustice was a widespread admiration for Mindszenty the man — especially when it was obvious that he had known before his arrest what fate awaited him in a Communist prison. Widespread world publicity was given to the statement he had penned three days before his arrest: "I have nothing to confess and I won't sign anything. If you should ever read that I have confessed or resigned, and even see it authenticated by my signature, remember that it will have been only the result of human frailty. In advance, I declare all such actions null and void."

This courageous leader and Prince of the Church, always

prepared for martyrdom, was not frightened. He did not feel sorry for himself. He had the knowledge and foresight to unmask the Communists' deceit with this pre-arrest document predicting that he would be deprived of his mind and will, and obliged to make "confessions" incompatible with his life and character.

Many people followed the news of the crooked trial with sympathy, others with admiration, all wondering where the Cardinal derived the spiritual stamina for such a superhuman ordeal. It is easy to see, looking back on his past life, how Divine Providence had led Cardinal Mindszenty through the vicissitudes of a hard life and prepared him well for his moment of truth. He had lived a life of discipline and difficult decisions. Two previous imprisonments (by Communist and Nazi tyrants) had not crushed him. His virtues had been hardened like steel in the furnace of sacrifice and suffering. His heroic character was based on an unshakable faith and hope in God, love for his Church and country, unassuming and humble demeanor, and steadfast loyalty to his principles and his people.

The Free World press, especially the Catholic press, made a conscientious effort to report not only the events of the mock trial, but also the Cardinal's extraordinary character and virtues. Millions of readers throughout the world became aware that the drama unfolding in Budapest revealed a new kind of living martyrdom, previously unknown in the 2,000-year history of Christianity.

The mock trial demonstrated that the new Communist executioners did not merely torture their victims to death. Instead, they first tried to demoralize them totally, squeezing out of their spirit even the heroism of martyrdom. In this one historic moment in Budapest, the whole world got a good look at the sinister face of Communism. What Cardinal Mindszenty had hoped and prayed for came to pass, namely, that his ordeal would alert the non-Communist world to this terrible threat to all Christian and Western civilization.

The worldwide Communist propaganda apparatus was badly hurt by Cardinal Mindszenty's mock trial. Communist Party bosses in other countries were acutely embarrassed. This is why the Hungarian Government moved rather quickly after two weeks to show the Cardinal to his mother and to Dr. Béla Witz.

Mother Mindszenty wrote a letter on March 3, 1949 to a friend in New York City describing this first visit to her imprisoned son, which took place on February 23: "I went to see him last week but was only allowed to say a few words. No one else is allowed to visit him, and he is not allowed to receive any mail or parcels. I don't know what will happen to him or how long they will keep him. I think often of the many kind Americans who have been so generous in sending us sympathy and gifts. I am very worried about the future and can stand the strain only because I know you are praying for me."[5]

In spite of the pessimism this letter reveals, Mother Mindszenty wasted no time in trying to get another visitor's permit. Her lawyer Dr. Farkas, Sister Elizabeth and I, all went to the authorities begging that she be allowed to see the Cardinal. Most of our requests were not even acknowledged. If the Communist bosses deigned to listen at all, their answer invariably was that they had to wait "until the trial's verdict became legally valid." They indicated that, only then, might she be permitted to visit him once every three months.

Mother Mindszenty couldn't wait. In April she went to Budapest to call on the bureaucrats and personally press them further. In another letter to her friend in New York City, she wrote on May 22, 1949:

"Having had no news, I was really worried. I went to Budapest on April 26, but did not get any chance to talk with Joseph. I was not even allowed to see him. To make a wasted journey of 150 miles each way is not easy for a woman of 75. I am heartbroken. I pray constantly, not knowing anywhere else to turn. I beg Jesus and His Blessed Mother to ease my bitterness and to help me carry this cross."

On July 6, 1949, the National Council of the People's Courts approved the February 8 verdict which had con-

demned Cardinal Mindszenty to life imprisonment. Only after
the Ministry of Justice released this news did Mother Mindszenty receive word that she might visit her son on July 25
and on the 25th of each month thereafter. This appeared to be
a great favor, but it was actually window dressing for the
Communists' future plans.

On July 25, Mother Mindszenty found the Cardinal in
his prison cell in fairly good health. She immediately relayed
this news to those of us who kept in close contact with her.
On August 25, however, she left the prison very disheart-
ened. She told us that the Cardinal appeared broken, depressed, and sick. ("Prison regulations" required the Cardinal
to stand during the entire time of all his mother's visits.)
Because of the short time they had together, they did not
even discuss his illness. She realized that she would have to
wait a whole month to question him further about his health.
After this visit, she wrote to her New York City friend:

"I was in Budapest to see my son. He is still alive, but is
very broken. He does not look well. I can visit him on the
25th of next month. I wish they would permit me more
visits."

Before her September visit, we talked to the Cardinal's
longtime personal physician, Dr. Ernest Pethő. From Mother
Mindszenty's description of the Cardinal's depression, Dr.
Pethő concluded that the Cardinal's former Basedow's disease (a thyroid gland illness) might have returned. The
doctor was rather surprised at a recurrence of its symptoms,
as there had been none whatsoever since his surgery more
than 15 years before. When we asked if this illness could
have been deliberately aggravated, he was silent; but the
expression on his face said clearly that it could.

Dr. Pethő advised Mother Mindszenty how to verify the
symptoms by opening his collar and finding out if his thyroid
gland were enlarged. He also authorized her to tell the prison
officials that he had been the Cardinal's doctor for years and
would be glad to perform any necessary surgery.

With considerable concern, we waited for the result of
her next visit. Mother Mindszenty went to Budapest several
days ahead of time to talk over the matter with friends. She

The Central Prison in Budapest. After the mock trial, the Cardinal's mother was finally allowed to visit him at this prison on February 23, 1949, July 25, 1949, August 25, 1949, and September 25, 1949. In the spring of 1954 when he was gravely ill, he was put in the hospital of this prison.

stayed in the Convent of the Sisters of Mercy of Szatmár.

On September 25, she arrived early at the prison gate. Waiting for her in the reception room was the same secret police agent who was always present at their meetings. The door opened and a tired, dejected Cardinal entered. He was so listless in talking with her that she asked, "Joseph, aren't you glad that I came to see you?" He limply said that he was quite sick, that his old Basedow's disease had returned, and that the pressure on his heart from an enlarged thyroid gland made him quite nervous. She opened his collar, touched his neck, and asked him if he had received any medical treatment. He said a doctor had given him a very superficial examination several weeks before, but he had never received any treatment.

Mother Mindszenty then asked the secret policeman why the prison officials had not given her son medical care. He did not answer. She asked him to inform prison officials that she would gladly pay all the medical expenses and, if surgery were necessary, that the Cardinal's physician, who was chief of staff at the Szombathely Hospital, would perform the operation.

Turning to the Cardinal, she said, "What do you think? Should we write a letter to the Government for permission to let Dr. Pethő examine you?" The Cardinal asked, "Do you really think they would permit an outside doctor to treat a prisoner?"

After her visit, she went to Szombathely to confer with Dr. Pethő. The doctor concluded that the Cardinal's Basedow's disease had indeed returned and that he needed immediate medical attention. He urged us to relay this message to the appropriate authorities, either orally or by letter, as the professional judgment of the Cardinal's longtime physician.

Mother Mindszenty and I proceeded to the Seminary to discuss a plan of action with Monsignor Géfin. The consensus was that she should write two letters: one to the Minister of Justice, the other to Archbishop Grősz, chairman of the Bishops' Conference. In the first, she would tell the Minister her impressions of her son's health and would urgently request medical care, as recommended by Dr. Pethő. In her second letter, she would also describe the Cardinal's condition and ask Archbishop Grősz, in his capacity as chairman of the Bishops' Conference, to send an official letter to the Government urging that the Cardinal be given immediate medical attention. She also asked him, in addition to his own letter, to forward her letter to the Minister of Justice, Stephen Riesz.

The next day she returned to Mindszent and sent me as courier to deliver the two letters she had written. At the train station, I spotted a secret police agent who had followed me several times before. To throw him off the track, I did not buy a ticket for Kalocsa through Budapest, which was the fastest route, but instead bought a ticket for Zalaegerszeg. There, I changed to an express for Pécs, and there boarded a train for Baja. I did not arrive in Kalocsa until the morning of October 15, after a two-day journey.

Archbishop Grősz received me immediately. He sat down at his typewriter and personally typed a letter to the Minister of Justice. He read it aloud to me, asking if it were exactly what we wanted. In his letter, he related the information about the Cardinal's health, based on the personal observations of his mother and Dr. Pethő's diagnosis. Then the Archbishop called the Minister's attention to prison regulations guaranteeing adequate medical care for prisoners. In the name of the Bishops' Conference, he asked that the Cardinal Primate of Hungary be given immediate medical attention. He added in his final paragraph that, if he did not receive prompt assurance that the Cardinal would receive the medical care guaranteed by the Republic's laws, he would publicly expose the callous attitude of the prison officials. Archbishop Grősz's letter was delivered to the Minister of Justice on October 16, 1949.

From this time on, no one knew the Cardinal's whereabouts. He disappeared without a trace. The Communists spread the story that he was taking a rest in the Mátra or the Tátra mountains, that he was under the care of Hungarian and Russian doctors, and that he had undergone a successful operation. Later, more alarming rumors were spread that Cardinal Mindszenty was critically ill and in great pain.

The Government cancelled the permit for his mother's visits. When she faithfully appeared at the prison on November 25 and referred to the permit granted in July, she was told abruptly that it was now null and void. She returned home, completely dejected and alarmed. After her November trip to Budapest, she wrote her New York City friend:

"My heart aches so much for my son who is suffering in prison. I commend him constantly to the protection of the Sacred Heart and the Blessed Mother. I am terribly depressed since my return from Budapest. I don't know what their reasons are, but they didn't let me see him or even give him a letter or package."

A few days later she wrote another letter to New York: "My life is filled with bitterness and tears. A 76-year-old mother, who is nearer the grave than to life, is not even allowed to see her son."

In December she did not go to Budapest, knowing that the long and tiresome journey would surely be in vain. She tried to mail the Cardinal a Christmas gift. She hoped that Dr. Farkas or Sister Elizabeth might be able to persuade the bureaucrats to forward the package. Despite their many connections, however, they were unsuccessful. The Communists' cruel behavior frightened her even more, and she feared that the reports about the Cardinal's transfer to Siberia or death might be true. A letter written on January 12, 1950 reveals how she suffered from this uncertainty:

"For me, the New Year brings only sorrow. The next month will be just like the last. I have lost hope that I will ever see my son again. I last talked with him on September 25, but since then I have neither seen nor heard from him. The radio has spread a rumor that he has been sent to Siberia. I don't know whether this is true or not. Since I have lost my son, nothing can console me. Cruel fate has snatched him from my arms. What can I do? I must resign myself."

CHAPTER 11

The Sixteenth of June

We were increasingly suspicious that the Communists had deliberately neglected the Cardinal's thyroid condition in order to exacerbate a recurrence of his illness. They refused treatment despite their certain knowledge that this condition had required surgery some years before. This would be such a simple way to dispose of the "Mindszenty problem"! The Communists could easily announce that the Cardinal's illness had returned due to the strain of the last several years, and that he had died of "natural causes." Certainly it was easy to believe that the public controversy, the interrogation, and the trial had taken their toll.

It was clear to us that his mother's once-a-month visits were carefully calculated to advance this cynical objective. The Communists shrewdly envisioned the simple peasant woman openly lamenting to all her friends how her son's health was steadily deteriorating. Our chilling conclusion was that the Communists were using Mother Mindszenty as their instrument to prepare public opinion to accept the Cardinal's death from "natural causes."

Archbishop Grősz and the rest of the Bishops shared our opinion and therefore, every time they met, they faithfully filed an official inquiry about the Primate's health. Archbishop Grősz even made several personal requests for a visitor's permit. These requests were invariably refused on the ground that only family members could visit a prisoner, which in this case meant only the Cardinal's mother.

Mother Mindszenty's friends discouraged her from making useless trips to Budapest during the severe winter months, but we made sure that she flooded the Government with inquiries as to the Cardinal's whereabouts. Even so, there was no word whether he was dead or alive.

Meanwhile, reports about the Cardinal's poor health circulated all over Hungary. Foreign radio stations repeated the same rumors, sometimes even announcing his death. During one bitter cold spell, Mother Mindszenty became so disturbed that she prepared to leave for Budapest anyway. We did not dare let her go because her asthma was sure to be aggravated by such a hard journey.

Knowing her temperament, we were sure that she would go to Budapest anyway just as soon as the weather barely permitted. We therefore looked around for a suitable companion for her trips to Budapest, and Sister Elizabeth's religious Superior was kind enough to make Sister Adelaide available for as much time as was necessary.

Sister Adelaide was born in Budapest and had attended high school and college there. She had worked in several of the convents and was well suited for the task of assisting Mother Mindszenty. Beginning in early 1950, she made many trips to Mindszent and carried numerous messages back and forth from there to Budapest and Szombathely.

Prison regulations at that time permitted prisoners to be visited once every three months. Mother Mindszenty was denied her three-month permission in December 1949. When six months rolled around without any word, she made a special plea to see the Cardinal on March 19, the feast of St. Joseph. Although she received no reply, she left for Budapest anyway on March 12 with Sister Adelaide and stayed at the Convent as before. I came from Szombathely to join them.

After getting Dr. Farkas' advice, Mother Mindszenty and Sister Adelaide went to plead with all the officials and bureaucrats who would see them. The authorities gave them no answer and refused even to allow them to send the Cardinal a package.

I could not miss my lectures at the Theological Seminary and after three days had to return to Szombathely. As the weather was now pleasant and the Sisters were always gracious hostesses, Mother Mindszenty decided to remain in Budapest for at least ten days.

Meanwhile, Sister Adelaide's elderly father was hospitalized and, at the end of March, she asked me to escort the Cardinal's mother home, which I did. As the train was passing through Győr, Mother Mindszenty told me that while in Budapest she had ordered a statue of the Sacred Heart for her parish church in Mindszent. She had discussed in detail the pose and measurements of the statue with the sculptor.

When he discovered he was dealing with Cardinal Mindszenty's mother, the sculptor gave her a very reasonable price. But even 1,500 forints was a large sum for her in 1950, a period of rapid inflation artificially caused by the Communists. Knowing it was a great sacrifice for her to pledge this sum, I told her that her friends would help her pay for the statue. She refused, saying she wanted to pay for it alone as her gift to the church in Mindszent. She added:

"You see, Father, I know now that my grief will have no human relief. Those who could help me won't, and those who want to help me, can't. I put my trust only in the Sacred Heart of Jesus, and I ask Him, if He finds me worthy, to reward my sacrifice by keeping my son alive and by letting me see him in prison."

Her bitter disappointments are revealed in this April 11, 1950 letter to her friend in New York City:

"I have been a long time in sending you this letter. I put off writing in the hope I might have some good news. But they would not let me see him and I have no information on where he is. I spent two weeks in Budapest and made request after request to the Government officials. I went personally to see them, but they would not receive me. A 76-year-old mother travels 150 miles by train to see her son and can't even find out if he is dead or alive. I returned with a heavy heart."

When Sister Adelaide returned to Szombathely after her father's funeral, she brought word that Cardinal Mindszenty was alive and that his mother should immediately appeal to John Pesti, the official in the Ministry of Justice who was in

charge of prisons. We helped Mother Mindszenty get ready
for this journey and chose May 25 as a good date for her to
present her request.

To our surprise, she was actually received by Pesti, who
confirmed that the Cardinal was indeed alive and in good
health. When she hinted about a permit for an immediate
visit, Pesti told her to be patient for a while, since certain
preparations had to be made for such a visit. He recommended that she return home and wait there for the permission. He agreed to forward to the Cardinal a parcel and a
rather large photograph of his mother. After eight months of
waiting, Mother Mindszenty returned from this interview im-
mensely relieved.

She arrived back home just about the time that the statue
of the Sacred Heart was delivered. The solemn dedication
took place on the feast of the Sacred Heart which in 1950
was on June 16. The clergy from the nearby villages and
towns came in impressive numbers, accompanied by many of
their parishioners. The church was filled to capacity, with an
overflow of hundreds outside and in the town square.

Examinations at the Theological Seminary prevented my
attending the dedication. It was nearly noon when I was
called to the phone. The pastor in Mindszent was calling to
tell me that Mother Mindszenty had received a telegram
granting permission to visit her son the next day. The telegram ordered her to go to the Ministry of Justice the very
next morning. The pastor had already checked the train
schedule, and he asked that Sister Adelaide and I come by
bus to Mindszent that afternoon and accompany Mother
Mindszenty to Celldömölk, where we would change for
another train to Budapest. On this schedule, we would arrive
in the capital by 5 o'clock in the morning.

I immediately called Sister Adelaide and she met me on
the bus. In Mindszent, we joined the Cardinal's mother, as
the pastor had planned.

Naturally I was curious about the telegram. Mother Mindszenty said Archbishop Grősz had sent it. Apparently, the
Government had chosen to grant the permission through
him. She told me that the telegram was handed to her the

moment she left the church after the dedication of her statue
in honor of the Sacred Heart.

In Zalabér we waited for the train for more than an hour.
When it finally arrived, I stepped into the first car and saved
three seats. Then I helped the women onto the train and
handed them the baggage through the window. Before re-
boarding the train, I caught sight of a young man who had
alighted from the last car. When he saw me (I was dressed
in a cassock), he hurried and boarded our car, taking a seat
just in front of us. Since we were so frequently followed by
secret police agents, I concluded that he was our guard.

As the train pulled out of the station, I began to read my
breviary, but soon realized that the women were talking
frankly about the Cardinal and the coming visit. I interrupted
them and suggested that they recite the Rosary. Our guard
could hear everything and certainly must have suspected my
reasons for diverting the women into prayer. The next moment he lay down on his bench to take a nap. He asked
Sister Adelaide (who was in secular clothes) to wake him up
in Celldömölk. He said he had had to work all day long
even though his mother's funeral was scheduled for the next
day. Within two minutes he was snoring.

At the terminal in Celldömölk, Sister Adelaide wanted
to wake him up, but I told her not to bother, he would waken
by himself. He did. He followed us from the train to the
waiting room. When we put down our luggage and sat
down, he departed. Five minutes later, a uniformed employee
of the railroad arrived to ask us: "Father, where are you
going, and what train are you waiting for?" I told him we
knew where we were going as well as the schedule, and we
would take the train we wanted. This happened about 9:00
P.M. and our train was scheduled to leave at 9:30.

The railroad official left, but a few moments later two

other men appeared in the waiting room. One secret police
agent, disguised as a painter, walked up and down in front
of us. He carried an easel and a box of paints. The other
secret police agent pretended to be a mechanic and carried a
small bag of tools. He remained quiet and rather near us,
either sitting on his tools or leaning against the wall. From
time to time, the railroad official popped his head through
the door, and then the "painter" or the "mechanic", or sometimes both, went to talk with him. A woman came into the
room, behaving as if she did not know the others. I soon
realized that both the "railroad official" and the woman were
part of the secret-police surveillance operation.

The train from Szombathely was quite late. When at last
we thought we heard it, Sister Adelaide hurried toward the
front of the station to make sure. The "painter," the "mechanic" and the woman followed her and surrounded her
outside the waiting room. Joined by the "railroad official",
they asked her our destination. She told them "Budapest."

Hearing this, the "railroad official" told Sister Adelaide
that he knew me from Zalaegerszeg and regretted my being
so reticent, since he had merely wanted to warn me that this
very night all priests in the country were to be arrested. Six
nights before, he said, the police had seized at least 1,000
religious men and women from their monasteries and convents and sent them to concentration camps in eastern Hungary. Sister Adelaide was terribly frightened at what he said,
but didn't tell me until the next day what the "railroad
official" had told her.

When the train finally arrived, the three of us entered a
third-class compartment for non-smokers. The "railway official" offered to help us, but I declined, saying that our luggage was not heavy. After we sat down, the "painter," the
"mechanic," and the woman all joined us in our compartment. The woman seated herself next to Mother Mindszenty,
and the two men sat on either side of the compartment
entrance. There were not many other passengers, probably
because our compartment was for non-smokers.

Anyone who wanted to smoke had to go into the aisle,
which the "painter," the "mechanic," and the woman all did

Cardinal Mindszenty's Mother on May 24, 1950. Father Joseph Vecsey is on the right. Sister Adelaide is standing.

at various intervals. When I went out into the corridor for a smoke, the "painter" and the "mechanic" both jumped up to offer me a match and start a conversation. I moved away from them, which probably indicated to them that I saw through their rather obvious maneuvers.

We arrived in Győr after midnight. There I looked for an unoccupied second-class compartment and convinced Mother Mindszenty that we should take it. I asked Sister Adelaide to go to the ticket office and pay the higher price, as we held only third-class tickets. When we picked up our luggage and Sister Adelaide left the train, our companions evidently became confused. The "painter" and the "mechanic" followed Sister, while the policewoman kept us under surveillance.

When Sister Adelaide returned, we moved to the second-class compartment and our companions disappeared. I hoped we would be left alone; Mother Mindszenty needed some rest after her strenuous festivities in Mindszent. I was tired, too, because we had had examinations at the Seminary all week. But during those early morning hours, a waiter interrupted us repeatedly. Every 15 or 20 minutes he would open our compartment door with a loud noise and offer us a drink or sandwiches. I still remember his malicious, sneering face at 3 A.M., opening our door with a tremendous bang and shouting like crazy, "Service!"

We got off the train at Budapest's Eastern Station. It was so early in the morning that we waited a while in the station. The "painter", the "mechanic" and the policewoman all sat opposite us in the waiting room. They appeared well-washed, well-dressed and rested.

Finally, we decided to take a streetcar to the Convent of the Sisters of Mercy of Szatmár and hope they would let us in, despite the very early hour. Our guards took the same streetcar and followed us all the way to the Convent. When we went inside, they vanished.

CHAPTER 12

Visitation at Vác

We had been at the Convent only a short while that morning of June 17, 1950 when Mother Mindszenty received a telegram ordering her to report to John Pesti, the prison official in the Ministry of Justice. Before she left, I said Mass in the Convent chapel. The nuns were glad for the chance to pray with the Cardinal's mother for his safety. During breakfast we planned her day.

Mother Mindszenty and Sister Adelaide left promptly, but it wasn't long until Sister returned alone. She and Mother Mindszenty had been received courteously at the Ministry and escorted up the elevator to Pesti's office on the fourth floor. There they were surprised to find Bishop Nicholas Dudás of the Eastern-rite diocese of Hajdudorog. He said he had been summoned to hear Cardinal Mindszenty's confession.

Mother Mindszenty immediately expressed the fear that this meant her son was ill. "No, no," the Bishop reassured her. "He is quite well." He told her that he had heard the Cardinal's confession in January and at that time got the impression that all symptoms of previous illness were gone.

At exactly 9:00 A.M. John Pesti entered the room and said that automobiles were waiting at the main entrance to the building. Mother Mindszenty got into one car, accompanied by two security guards, a man and a woman. Bishop Dudás rode in the other car with two policemen. Sister Adelaide was not allowed to go with them, so she returned to the Convent on Délibáb Street.

I spent an anxious morning praying for the success of Mother Mindszenty's mission. By noon, my anticipation was so keen that I was pacing up and down at the Convent door. When she finally arrived at 12:30, her first words were:

"Joseph is alive and well, thanks be to God." She then gave me a step-by-step account of her morning's experiences.

She had assumed she would be taken to the Central Prison in Budapest where she had previously seen the Cardinal. When she saw the cars heading in a different direction, she showed her surprise and asked her guards if they were driving to Vác. The guards pretended they did not hear her question. Later, as the car drove northeast out of the city, she again whispered her question to the woman guard, who remained silent.

As Mother Mindszenty suspected, the cars drove to Vác and pulled up in front of the prison there. She and Bishop Dudás were taken to a visiting room on the third floor. After a few moments, a door on the opposite side opened and the Cardinal entered with a guard at his side. The Cardinal embraced his mother warmly and gave Bishop Dudás the kiss of peace, as it is given during Mass.

The Cardinal's guard then announced that he had permission for a 30-minute visit with his mother, plus 15 minutes with the Bishop for confession. Bishop Dudás was told to leave the room, while the guard remained to supervise the Cardinal's conversation.

For the first time, the guard permitted the Cardinal to sit down during a visit with his mother. He seemed healthy and reasonably content. He wore a neat black suit with a Roman collar, which was a big change from previous visits. Mother Mindszenty told him, "Joseph, your suit and shoes are in very good condition. I was afraid they would be ragged after being worn for a year and a half!"

The Cardinal responded jokingly, "Mother, you know that children are always washed and dressed up for visitors."

Later we realized that the Communists had cleverly contrived this prison visit to create the impression that they had been treating the captive Cardinal humanely. He knew perfectly well what they were doing, but did not dare explain it to his mother with the guard standing right next to them. The Communists arranged this visit in order to mislead the Cardinal's mother and, through her, the public. Mother Mindszenty was convinced that her son was being well treated.

Although she noticed that he was quite thin, she made herself believe this was because he had voluntarily fasted in prison. We who were close to her and to whom she described this visit were similarly misled.

The truth, however, was quite different. When I saw Cardinal Mindszenty on November 1, 1956 after the Hungarian Freedom Fighters had liberated him from prison, he personally told me he was treated so badly that "even today, I do not know where I spent those four years after I was transferred from the first prison."

Based on information I obtained from numerous other prisoners, plus the Cardinal's critical illness in the fourth year of his imprisonment, I concluded that he was kept in the prison on Conti Street in the 8th district of Budapest. This notorious prison had the reputation of being a jail where political prisoners were assured of an early death from "natural causes." Each time the Communists permitted the Cardinal to have a visit from his mother, he was driven from the Conti Street prison to Vác in order to deceive her, and through her the public, about the treatment he was receiving.

Not knowing this at the time, and remembering how depressed her son was at their previous meeting, Mother Mindszenty returned to the Convent happy that he was healthy and in good spirits. When she asked him how he spent his days in prison, he said he made daily meditations, said Mass and his Divine Office, recited the Rosary six times, and read extensively in his Bible. He told her he was permitted to take short walks. With the guard standing right there, the Cardinal could not tell her what he told me later: that for four long years, his "walks" had been confined to a tiny area surrounded by high walls where no sunlight ever penetrated.

The Cardinal asked his mother about family affairs, about his sisters and their children and grandchildren. He also asked about her vineyard and orchard, and if she still did all her own chores. He asked how she came to Vác.

"From Budapest it was easy," she said, "because the Minister of Justice sent me in a car. However, from our home to Budapest, I had to travel all night by a very slow train. I didn't have time to prepare a package for you because I had

to leave immediately after receiving the telegram granting
permission for this visit. I was able to bring you something
from the special dinner we had after the dedication of the
new statue at our church, but the Minister of Justice made
me leave that package with him. He said he would deliver
it to you."

Of course, she told the Cardinal about the new statue of
the Sacred Heart of Jesus which she had given in thanksgiving for the Lord's help through so many difficult months. She
said that she obviously had to be in good health in order to
make so many exhausting trips to Budapest! Within the last
year, she had made eight journeys to the capital, four of them
in vain.

She told the Cardinal how she appreciated the way the
professors at the Szombathely Seminary had assisted her on
these trips and often accompanied her. She told him that I
(as Prefect of the Seminary) had to be home for an ordination of priests the very next day, and that she wanted to be
there too, "since this month, Joseph, will be the 35th anniversary of your own ordination in that same beautiful
Cathedral."[1]

Mother Mindszenty told me that the Cardinal was touched
by her news and asked her to relay his promise that he would
say his Mass the next day for the newly-ordained priests, and
that he sent his blessings to everyone at the Seminary.

The allotted 30 minutes passed quickly. The guard looked
at his watch and gave the sign to admit Bishop Dudás. As
soon as the Bishop entered, he told the Cardinal the sad
news that the Cardinal's Vicar General, Monsignor John
Drahos, who had been administering the Esztergom Archdiocese since the Cardinal's arrest, had died the previous
night. (According to Canon Law, Vicar General Drahos
automatically became the head of the Archdiocese after the
Cardinal's arrest, and was later appointed titular Bishop.)

With Mother Mindszenty and Bishop Dudás standing
there, the Cardinal expressed his sympathy, as well as his
concern for the future of his Archdiocese. He closed the subject by saying that the Archdiocesan Canons had the responsi-

bility for making a new appointment. Mother Mindszenty was then returned to her car and driven back to the Convent on Délibáb Street.

Immediately after this visit, the Communists circulated the rumor in Budapest that Cardinal Mindszenty had sent a message to the Canons in Esztergom through Bishop Dudás. This spurious message was supposed to have urged the Canons to elect Monsignor Nicholas Beresztóczy as Vicar General of the diocese.

Of course, this was a Communist fabrication. Bishop Dudás never told anyone that Cardinal Mindszenty wanted Beresztóczy elected as Vicar. Bishop Dudás was well aware of the fact that Beresztóczy was a Communist fellow traveler.

Because I had already suspected that there was some connection between Bishop Dudás' visit and Monsignor Drahos' death the day before, I had questioned Mother Mindszenty very carefully on this point as soon as she returned from her visit. From her answers, it was clear that she was present during the entire conversation between the Cardinal and Bishop Dudás. She had joined attentively in the discussion as she had known Monsignor Drahos rather well. She told me emphatically that no name of a possible successor was mentioned either by the Cardinal or by Bishop Dudás, and that it was utterly impossible that such a discussion took place during the few moments of the Cardinal's confession.

A year and a half before, Monsignor Beresztóczy had been arrested by the secret police and tortured in their headquarters at 60 Andrássy Street. He was kept in prison for several months and released in the spring of 1949 on condition that he would do whatever the Communists wanted him to do.

It was obvious that the Government wanted the election of the terror-stricken Monsignor Beresztóczy in order that the Communists themselves could administer Cardinal Mindszenty's own Archdiocese of Esztergom. The Communists evidently summoned Bishop Dudás to see Cardinal Mindszenty so that this visit could be cleverly used to spread the false rumor that the Cardinal wanted Beresztóczy elected Vicar.

Among those who spread this falsehood was Matthias Rákosi, the Secretary of the Hungarian Communist Party. At that time, he headed a Government committee which was engaged in some negotiations with a committee of the Bishops' Conference. Rákosi took advantage of the June 28, 1950 meeting with some of the Bishops to feign indignation and charge:

"We cannot cope with this Mindszenty even in prison! On June 17 we allowed his mother to visit him and Bishop Dudás to hear his confession. And you see, Mindszenty used this opportunity to interfere in Church business! He actually sent a message through Bishop Dudás telling the Canons to elect Nicholas Beresztóczy as Vicar."

Under instructions from the Communists, Monsignor Beresztóczy campaigned for his own election. He wrote each Canon saying that Cardinal Mindszenty wanted him to be Vicar General and said the same thing orally when the Canons gathered for the election. As soon as he finished speaking, however, Auxiliary Bishop Zoltán Meszlényi read aloud Cardinal Mindszenty's last letter to the Canons, warning that after his arrest they were not to accept any statements or messages purporting to come from him. After this straightforward move by the Auxiliary, the Canons quickly elected Dr. Béla Witz on the first ballot. Frail and timid, Dr. Witz did not dare to accept the position of Vicar General of Esztergom because he knew the Communists were determined to secure that post for Beresztóczy.

On the second ballot, the Canons elected Auxiliary Bishop Dr. Zoltán Meszlényi. He governed the Esztergom Archdiocese for only two weeks. The Communists then arrested him on false charges and sent him to a concentration camp in Kistarcsa, where he died in the fourth year of his detention.

At the time that Bishop Meszlényi was arrested, the secret police searched the homes of several Canons. They were threatened with arrest and prison if they failed to vote for

Beresztóczy on the next ballot. By this brutal means, the Communists forced the Canons to elect Beresztóczy as Vicar at their next meeting.

It is not hard to understand why the Canons succumbed. Most of them were old or ill, or both. The two most eminent and likely candidates for Vicar, Dr. Charles Giegler and Julius Mátray, had been imprisoned as soon as the Communists heard about Vicar Drahos' seriously failing health. The three arrests, the terrorist series of house searches, and the brutal threats, explain the way the Canons finally caved in and elected Beresztóczy as Archdiocesan Vicar.

Such Communist tricks, however, were well known to Pope Pius XII. Beresztóczy was effectively displaced by the Pope's appointment of Andrew Hamvas, Bishop of Csanád, as Apostolic Administrator of the Esztergom Archdiocese. Unfortunately, this did not solve the problem. It was under this timid Bishop's administration that Cardinal Mindszenty's own Archdiocese was allowed to fall into the hands of the leftist "peace priests."

After Mother Mindszenty told me the details of her visit, we had to resume our traveling immediately if we were to attend the ordination scheduled for the following day. She took time only to greet a few visitors and give them the good news about the Cardinal.

By the middle of the afternoon, we were on our way to Szombathely. It was Saturday and the train was crowded with weekend passengers. We had a hard time finding one seat for Mother Mindszenty. We were afraid she might suffer an asthma attack, but fortunately her exhilaration overcame the physical strain.

At Györ several passengers got off, so Sister Adelaide and I found seats. Our hope for a rest was spoiled when a large number of secret police boarded at Pápa, taking every space in our compartment and carrying on a boisterous conversation. Mother Mindszenty said her prayers.

The secret police got off at Szombathely with us and quickly filled the last streetcar operating that night so that all other train passengers had to walk to their destinations. We walked about a mile to the Seminary. Sister Adelaide helped Mother Mindszenty, and I carried the luggage. It was shortly after midnight when we arrived. Monsignor Géfin had supper waiting for us.

The next morning Mother Mindszenty came to the ordination and, at the reception afterwards, personally told the newly-ordained priests that the Cardinal had offered his Mass for them and sent his blessing to each one. Afterwards, she was driven home to Mindszent in the ordaining Bishop's car.

The secret police who had boarded the train at Pápa had a reason for coming to Szombathely. The following night, on June 18, 1950, they raided the local religious houses and arrested about 100 priests and brothers and 300 nuns. Among the men arrested were Canons of Prémontré, Salesian Fathers, and priests of the Dominican and Franciscan Orders. The nuns arrested included Carmelites, Dominicans, Annunciate Sisters, Sisters of Social Service, and Daughters of Charity.

The same night there were similar raids throughout the country. About 1,000 priests, monks, brothers and nuns were dragged out of their monasteries and convents and deported to concentration camps in eastern Hungary. This was the second widespread attack on Catholic religious orders under the false charge that monasteries and convents were centers for weapons and spies sent into Hungary by the Western powers.

CHAPTER 13

The Agreement

With Cardinal Mindszenty out of the way after his mock trial, the Communist Government no longer feared an open confrontation with the Bishops. The Bishops felt that any forthright defense of religious freedom could easily precipitate large-scale persecution.

Archbishop Joseph Grősz of Kalocsa had succeeded to the chairmanship of the Bishops' Conference, and the Primate's responsibilities fell on his shoulders. Instead of open confrontation, the new chairman chose passive resistance. This decision was determined partly by his non-combative temperament, but more by the fact that he simply was not equipped with the superior leadership talents and organizational skill which had enabled Cardinal Mindszenty for nearly four years to successfully defend the rights of the Church and the religious freedom of the people.

The second most influential member of the Bishops' Conference was Archbishop Julius Czapik of Eger, who was nicknamed "the diplomat" by the "progressive Catholics." Later, after Archbishop Grősz was imprisoned, Archbishop Czapik became the chairman of the Bishops' Conference. His health was very poor, which undoubtedly influenced him to steer clear of any collision course with the Government's persecution of the Church. He dreaded prison, knowing that his failing strength could not stand the torture and suffering.

All this was well known to the Communists and they exploited the situation for their own anti-religious objectives. Archbishop Czapik's compromising attitude split the unity of the hierarchy. On the eve of the Mindszenty trial, for example, he had wanted to accept as authentic a forged letter allegedly from the Cardinal — despite the opposition of the majority of the Bishops' Conference. He also attended the

gala reception for the President of the Communist Government on February 1, 1949, although such attendance was
strongly opposed by the rest of the hierarchy. No doubt the
Communists counted on his further support on February 15,
1949 when they sent the Bishops' Conference another forged
letter supposedly from the Cardinal. Addressed to Archbishop Grösz, the forged letter read:[1]

"Your Excellency:

"Please ask the Minister of Justice to permit you or another Bishop to visit me so we can talk over my present
situation and other pertinent questions.

"For some 50 days, I have pondered the present situation
and groped for a solution, or at least a *modus vivendi*, for
Church-State relations. We should discuss certain basic con-
cepts for rapprochement which I have outlined in a letter to
the Minister of Justice[2] in order to pick up the thread for
future negotiations which would guarantee the doctrine, laws
and rights of the Church.

"Although in the past I did not choose a path of concilia-
tion, I would like now to earnestly support any efforts for
compromise. It is now clear to me that we formerly considered only our side of the case, without a real understanding
of the problems of Hungarian democracy.

"I want the Bishops' Conference to initiate negotiations
with the Government. I hope personally to be a real help in
the future. As I have already written to the Minister of
Justice, I consider it urgent that there be a just agreement
between the Church and the State. With all my energies, I
want to promote a policy of peace between Church and
State. Please forward this letter to Archbishop Czapik.

"With best wishes,
"Joseph Mindszenty"

The Bishops' Conference took up the matter of this
forged letter at its February 18, 1949 meeting and declared
that negotiations with the Government could be initiated only
with the Vatican's permission. The Communists were well
aware, of course, that after Cardinal Mindszenty's mock trial,
the Vatican would have nothing to do with them.

In the following months, the Communists stepped up their subtle forms of persecution. They took several anti-religious measures, one of the most offensive being the abolition of religious education in all schools. The Communists simply ignored the constitutional amendment, passed at the time the Catholic schools were expropriated a year earlier, which assured parents that religious education in all primary and secondary schools would continue.

During the attacks on the Catholic schools, Cardinal Mindszenty had repeatedly pointed out that the Communists were trying to put all private schools under Government control because they wanted to make them citadels of Marxist materialism, just as the public schools had already become. The Communist Government categorically denied those charges, pointing out that the Constitution had been amended to require the teaching of religion in the schools.

Now, however, in spite of the Constitution and all the solemn promises, the Government issued a regulation that the teaching of religion in all schools was abolished — unless requested by the individual parents.

This new regulation was made public just before the new school year opened in 1949. To the great surprise of the Government, 95 per cent of the students requested religious instruction. The Communists reacted quickly. They dispatched secret instructions to school officials on how to decrease the number of students requesting religious instruction. One method was to fire numerous religion teachers from the schools as "reactionaries." Another way was for teachers and principals to warn the students that, if they received religious instruction, they would not be admitted to higher studies, universities would be closed to them, and they would not be able to secure either scholarships or public financial aid.

A third method of "persuasion" was for militant Communist Party members to call on the parents at home or at work and "explain" to them the disadvantages of a religious education for their children.

Meanwhile, all non-Marxist youth organizations were dissolved, including the Boy and Girl Scouts and the YMCA. Their members were advised to join Marxist youth societies, which were hotbeds of anti-religious activity. All the textbooks in the schools were rewritten to conform to Marxist ideology. Students in State colleges were specifically forbidden to go to church or receive religious instruction. Those who applied for admission to any university had to take examinations which included anti-religious questions; if a student admitted he believed in God or was a church-goer, he simply was not accepted. Religious publishing houses were nationalized. Only Communists were permitted to publish books or periodicals designed for the ideological training of youth. Hungarian young people were inundated by anti-religious propaganda.

Catholic weekly newspapers were forced into the hands of the "progressives." Only "progressive Catholics" were allowed to give public lectures. Parrot-like, they reiterated the Party line that Catholics must live in "peaceful coexistence" with the Marxist parties and collaborate with them. Ignoring the stream of slanders against the Church, these "progressive Catholics" tried to convince the public that the tension between Church and State was caused by the "reactionary" and "anti-democratic" clergy.

University Extension programs giving religious instruction were restricted. Bible study groups were prohibited. The secret police began surveillance of all contacts between the clergy and their parishioners outside of church, including visits by lay apostles to families in their parishes.

The Bishops' Conference, in order to avoid provoking outright persecution, endured this situation without protest. At the beginning, the ideological danger was not too great, since most students found Marxist ideology ridiculous. Both adults and young people had their own opinions about the Communist regime and could easily see that Marxist morality contrasted most unfavorably with the Gospel and the Christian way of life. The Cardinal's heroic leadership, and the fidelity of the highly-educated and well-disciplined clergy and religious teachers who were inspired by his example, assured that the spiritual harm inflicted on the Church was not very great in the period immediately following the mock trial.

The Communists expelled the religious not only from their schools, but also from hospitals, orphanages and homes for the aged. The Bishops then transferred these religious into regular diocesan activities. The men were assigned as additional pastors or assistant pastors and to run retreat houses. The nuns were assigned to various pastoral duties; they gave religious instruction, ran rectory offices, served as sacristans and choir leaders, and did other parish work such as visiting homes and families in apartment projects.

When the Communists saw this impressive apostolic activity, they responded with calculated harassment. Local authorities did not dare to protect the religious from such harassment by the Communist Party and the secret police. The Superiors of the major religious orders, therefore, presented this petition to the Government on April 15, 1950 recounting their grievances and requesting redress:

"We have been squeezed into overcrowded ghetto-like quarters, after having been obliged to leave our convents, monasteries, and seminaries. In expropriating our schools, Government officials have gone far beyond what the law requires. They have confiscated our buildings, cloisters, courtyards, gardens, orchards, and equipment.

"Again going far beyond the law, in several cases officials have confiscated our chapels, retreat houses, cultural centers, and printing presses. They have restricted our missionary work, our retreats, our visiting of churches, our home visits, and our sick calls. They have seized our novitiates and our theological academies.

"They harass and obstruct individual religious on the slightest pretext. Professions open to others are closed to us. Over the objections of both doctors and patients, nurses who are nuns have been fired, having been informed they can keep their jobs only if they abandon convent life."[3]

The Government did not respond to this petition from the Superiors of the leading orders. The indirect word came back through the "progressive Catholics" that the Government would negotiate any and all Church-State problems only with the Bishops. When this message was given to Archbishop Grősz, he resolutely refused to initiate negotiations.

The Government then turned to violent tactics to force the Bishops to begin Church-State talks on Communist terms. In a night raid on June 9, 1950, the secret police arrested 1,000 religious (priests, monks, brothers and nuns) and put them in concentration camps. On June 17, the Superiors of the major religious orders presented this petition to Archbishop Grősz, urging him to protest to the Government in the name of the Bishops' Conference:

"No other grievance does the entire Catholic community feel more keenly than the events which have taken place in the last few days in southern Hungary. There, religious life is now *de facto* extinct. About 1,000 priests, monks, brothers and nuns — some sick and disabled, some more than 80 years old, some even cloistered with pontifical enclosure — have been removed from their monasteries and convents and forcibly deported to northern Hungary under the pretext that 'their presence is a danger to public order and security.'

"They have been herded together in ghetto-like quarters, without food or necessities. In many cases, they lack the most elementary necessities because their surprise deportation happened at night without any chance to make suitable preparations. Generally, they were given only 15 minutes to get ready. Consequently, many could not even dress properly.

"The treatment by the guards was often cruel and rude, offending human dignity and sometimes even human decency. When the general public heard about this night raid, and the next morning approached the former religious houses, the Government authorities uttered defamatory remarks about the religious, accusing them of crimes we had never heard of before."[4]

Archbishop Grősz still did not feel anything would be accomplished by resuming the Communist-style negotiations which the Bishops had terminated in 1949 under orders from Pope Pius XII. To break all remaining spirit of resistance by Archbishop Grősz and the Bishops' Conference, the Communists then seized another 1,000 religious men and women in a second night raid on June 18, 1950 and sent them also to concentration camps.

These two night raids made it clear that the Communists would use every cruelty to force the Bishops' Conference to accept dictation from the Government. The Communists used the "progressive Catholics" to spread the word that, if the Bishops did not immediately initiate negotiations, all the 2,000 priests, monks, brothers and nuns would be deported to Siberia. Archbishop Grősz was thus forced to capitulate. On June 20, 1950, he convened the Bishops' Conference which decided that the safety of the religious required them to negotiate with the Communist Government.

The delegates from the Bishops' Conference met with Government representatives on June 28, 1950. Archbishop Grősz made a statement listing the grievances of the religious orders, and Archbishop Czapik presented a motion to remedy these grievances. Rákosi, the General Secretary of the Communist Party, responded that the "affair of the religious orders" was only a secondary issue and that, if the Bishops remained unwilling to negotiate on more substantial matters and sign an agreement, the Government would continue the arrests. Rákosi presented a formal demand that delegates from the Bishops' Conference appear at the next meeting on July 5 with a written mandate to sign an agreement which would settle all Church-State problems.[5]

On July 5, the Bishops presented their position in 20 points. The first five asked for recognition of the independence and autonomy of the Church and the separation of Church and State. Points 6 through 17 asked the Government to remedy various grievous infringements of religious freedoms. Points 18 through 20 asked for recognition of the inalienable right of the Church to accept financial support from its members, and for some alleviation of the dire financial stress resulting from the confiscation of Church properties.

Rákosi answered: (1) All motions made by the Bishops' Conference had to be revised along the lines of the recent Church-State agreement made in Poland. (2) The Communist Government would have the right of veto over the nomination of bishops (as formerly exercised by the Hungarian kings). (3) All religious orders had to be dissolved immediately. (4) The interned priests, monks, brothers and nuns could leave the concentration camps as soon as they agreed to give up religious life and "return to the world." (5) The Government might contribute a small amount toward meeting the expenses incurred by the internees.[6]

At another meeting on July 12, the episcopal delegates again protested the dissolution of the religious orders, but nevertheless promised their cooperation in disbanding them. Rákosi then stated that, as a reward for the Bishops' "new attitude," the Government would (1) temporarily renounce its right of veto, (2) permit 400 priests who were members of religious orders to transfer into diocesan service, (3) permit three or four religious to live together in one household after dissolution of their orders, and (4) help place the sick and aged religious in public charity homes.[7]

On July 20 the Bishops' delegates also accepted the Government's terms that only two secondary schools could be maintained by each of only four religious orders: the Benedictines, the Piarist Fathers, the Franciscans, and the Sisters of Notre Dame of Szeged.

Shortly after, however, a Government decree ordered the dissolution of all religious orders. The monasteries for religious men were reduced from 187 to 6. Out of 456 convents for nuns, all but 2 were closed. Each remaining monastery and convent was restricted to a maximum of 25 members.

Thus, of the once-proud total of 3,122 Catholic schools, only eight remained — and these, as Rákosi wryly noted, were by temporary Government suffrage. Out of a once-proud total of 11,000 men and women who belonged to religious orders, only 200 could remain in the surviving monasteries and convents. Of the 2,500 priests who belonged to religious orders, only 400 were allowed to do pastoral work. Monasteries, convents, seminaries and novitiates had to be abandoned by December 31, 1950, the date set for Government confiscation of all their property and equipment.

By August 10, 1950, the Government felt it had disposed of the problem of the religious orders. On that day, the Government representatives handed over to the Bishops the prospective text of an "Agreement" between the Catholic Church and the State. In order to make sure that the Bishops signed the document, the Communists carried out last-minute menacing and brutal tactics, including searches of episcopal residences and the arrest of various chancery personnel.

The text of the "Agreement" was made public only on the day it was signed on August 30, 1950:

"The Government of the Hungarian People's Republic and the Conference of Catholic Bishops, moved by the sincere desire for peaceful coexistence between the State and the Catholic Church, and in order to promote the unity, prosperity and peaceful progress of our nation, have entered into mutually beneficial negotiations, and now make the following Agreement:

I.

"1. The Bishops' Conference recognizes that it is the Bishops' duty as citizens to support the Government and Constitution of the Hungarian People's Republic. It declares that it will, according to Church law, take measures against Church personnel who work against the Government and the peace and prosperity of the Hungarian People's Republic.

"2. The Bishops' Conference emphatically condemns as subversive all activity against the social order of the Hungarian People's Republic, whatever its purpose. It declares that for clergy to engage in such activity would be to pervert religion for political purposes.

"3. The Bishops' Conference appeals to the faithful, as citizens and patriots, to do their share in the Government's reconstruction projects and thereby achieve success for the Five Year Plan designed to increase the nation's living standard and promote social justice. The Bishops' Conference admonishes the clergy not to help the farmers to resist being organized into *kolkhozy* [collective farms], since these are voluntary associations based on the solidarity of the people.

"4. The Bishops' Conference supports the Peace Movement and approves the efforts of the People's Republic to maintain peace. It condemns warmongering, condemns nuclear weapons, and condemns their use as a crime against humanity.

II.

"1. The Government and the Constitution of the Hungarian People's Republic guarantee complete religious freedom for Catholics and assure the Catholic Church its freedom of activity.

"2. The Government of the Hungarian People's Republic approves the restoration to the Church of eight Catholic schools (six for boys and two for girls), and agrees that in these schools there be a sufficient number of teachers from religious orders.

"3. The Government of the People's Republic, according to the prior agreement made with the different religious bodies, is ready to take care of the material necessities of the Catholic Church to the extent that for 18 years (until the Church can cover its expenses from its own sources) the Government will make adequate payments for expenses incurred by the Church. These will be paid after three and five year periods in decreasing installments. As part of its financial responsibility, the People's Republic assures a minimum subsistence for the clergy.

"Execution of the above Agreement is placed in the hands of an equal number of delegates representing the Hungarian People's Republic and the Bishops' Conference."

According to Lenin, all religion must be completely subjected to the State. The objectives and tactics spelled out by Lenin were supplemented in Hungary by Communist Party boss Matthias Rákosi. He developed the famous technique which he later candidly described in a speech on February 29, 1952 as "salami tactics," that is, the cutting off of his opposition slice by slice.

In Hungary, the Communists accomplished their antireligious objective in two stages. First, religious denominations were deprived of all their properties, schools, organizations, press, and every social and cultural institution. They were isolated from the nation's social life. They were forbidden every contact with members of their faith in other countries.

In the second phase, religious leaders were removed from positions of influence in accordance with the maxim, "Strike the shepherd, and the sheep will be scattered." This Communist tactic was accomplished principally from within by organizing fellow travelers among some weaker priests and laymen who had been morally compromised, or who had difficulties with their superiors, and therefore could be recruited by force or trickery. Their insidious activities were vigorously promoted by the Communists from behind the scenes through the media, financial subsidies, and the secret police. A similar role had been played in the West Ukraine by what was called the "Living Church," and in the Ruthenian and Transylvanian parts of Hungary through such pro-Communist clerical groups as the "Orthodox Union Movement" and the "Priests' Peace Movement."

The Communists put Monsignor Nicholas Beresztóczy in charge of the Priests' Peace Movement. After the way he had been tortured and intimidated by the secret police in early 1949, the Government knew he was a reliable Communist collaborator.

On August 1, 1950, Beresztóczy held the first organizational meeting of the Priests' Peace Movement in Budapest. Assisting him were Father Stephen Balogh, a priest who had been a Communist collaborator from the beginning, and Father Richard Horváth, a suspended Cistercian monk. The Government sent to this meeting the Minister of Education who proposed that all present should request the Bishops' Conference to sign the Agreement with the Government and announce that they confined their allegiance to the Vatican solely to matters of faith and morals, and that they would follow their own consciences in all other matters.

Using brute force, the secret police recruited some 150 priests to attend this first meeting of the Peace Movement. This number would have been even less if all the bishops had forbidden their priests to attend. Some bishops gave no instructions at all. Others, such as Archbishop Czapik and Bishop Hamvas, left the decision to the individual priests. Only Archbishop Grősz of Kalocsa, Bishop Pétery of Vác, and Bishop Badalik of Veszprém forbade their priests to attend. However, when Bishop Pétery called four disobedient priests to account before an ecclesiastical panel, the priest judge and two other members of the panel were arrested by the secret police.

The invitation to join the Priests' Peace Movement was extended to every priest and seminarian in Hungary, but only 35 joined, which was only 0.5 per cent of the 7,000 Hungarian clergy. That this small number of priests should dare to speak in the name of the whole Catholic Church in Hungary looked strange even to the Communists. So, after the Church-State Agreement was signed, the Government's chief aim was to increase the number of "peace priests." When priests declined to join the Movement saying that their bishop did not want them to, the Communists pointed to the text of the Agreement as proof that the Bishops' Conference supported the Priests' Peace Movement.

The Bishops' Conference could not accept this interpretation of the Agreement. When certain "peace priests" issued statements revealing the anti-religious aims of the Peace Movement, the Bishops confidentially forbade their priests to take part. When the Communists learned of this, they used their priest-collaborators to publicly attack the Bishops' Conference, directing their invective particularly against Archbishop Grősz of Kalocsa, Bishop Joseph Pétery of Vác, Bishop Louis Shovy of Székesfehérvár, and Bishop Bartholomew Badalik of Veszprém. The Marxist press was full of such attacks, and beginning in November 1950, the weekly publication of the Peace Movement, called *The Cross*, specialized in denunciations. In spite of all such attacks, the Communists never succeeded in recruiting any significant number of priests into the Priests' Peace Movement.

Mother Mindszenty was greatly concerned about the hardships suffered by the religious and also by the way the Communists had so cleverly humiliated the Bishops' Conference. She prayed daily for the persecuted Church – in the morning at Mass and later on while working in her vineyard. Her only comfort was to know that the Cardinal was still alive in prison. Her hope and trust in God and her strong will were never broken, not even in her most trying months.

Sister Adelaide, who spent several weeks in Mindszent during the summer of 1950, spoke enthusiastically about Mother Mindszenty's great spiritual strength. As Sister Adelaide lived and worked right along with Mother Mindszenty in the kitchen and in the vineyard, she was able to observe her very closely. The indefatigable Mother Mindszenty cooked the meals for all those who worked in her fields, and then worked in the vineyard herself the rest of the day.

Mother Mindszenty talked freely about her son, and never seemed nervous or hurried. She waited patiently for another permit to visit the Cardinal, relying on the prison officials' adhering to the regulations which allowed each prisoner a visit every three months. She confidently expected another opportunity during September.

At the end of August, Sister Adelaide carried to Budapest a letter from Mother Mindszenty addressed to John Pesti in which she humbly referred to the fact that September 17, 1950 would mark three months from the date of her last visit, and she asked permission for a visit that month. Her lawyer, Dr. Farkas, personally delivered the letter to Pesti's office in the Ministry of Justice, but received no answer. She sent another request after the middle of September, again receiving no reply. In October she finally turned to Archbishop Grősz to intervene for her with the Government.

I personally delivered her letter to the Archbishop in Budapest just before the opening of a session of the Bishops' Conference. I also asked him to make a request in the name of the Bishops that the Cardinal's mother be granted her regular three-month permit. I explained how difficult it was for this elderly woman living in the country to have to deliver every request for visitation rights to the Ministry of Justice and to be forced, in effect, to lobby repeatedly in the Budapest offices of various Party functionaries.

After the Bishops' Conference, the Archbishop forwarded an account of the entire problem to the Government, but received no reply. Finally, he was informed that there was no need for his intercession because the Cardinal's mother regularly obtained permission to visit her son in accordance with prison regulations. Archbishop Grősz sent the Government's answer to Mother Mindszenty, whereupon she inferred that she could obtain her permit every three months if she appeared personally at the Ministry of Justice.

I accompanied her to Budapest on November 10. We stayed at the Central Major Seminary. After the dissolution of the religious orders, the Rector of this Seminary, Father Michael Marcell, a friend of the Cardinal, gave Mother Mindszenty overnight hospitality whenever she came to Budapest. Sister Adelaide was available, since she lived with her mother in Budapest after her religious order was dissolved.

The next day, Mother Mindszenty and Sister Adelaide went to see John Pesti in his office. He coolly told them that, since the last visit, prison regulations had been changed, and prisoners could now receive visitors only every six months. Mother Mindszenty had a sad trip back home, especially so because the radio was once again broadcasting stories about the Cardinal's poor health.

On November 27, Pesti sent word to Mother Mindszenty that she could see the Cardinal on November 30, 1950. The very next day she came to Szombathely, and on November 29 I accompanied her to Budapest. On the train to Budapest we talked about some of the questions she might ask the Cardinal in order that we could figure out his daily schedule, treatment, and exactly where he was imprisoned.

On November 30, joined by Sister Adelaide, she went to the Ministry of Justice. As in June, Mother Mindszenty was driven to Vác in a car with a male and female member of the secret police. She saw the Cardinal in the same room at the Vác prison where they had visited before.

When she returned to the Central Major Seminary where we were staying, she gave me a full report on her long-awaited visit. Following the line of questioning we had worked out ahead of time, she had asked the Cardinal, "Do you really have a chance to celebrate Holy Mass every day?"

"Yes, Mother. I say Mass every day — except I didn't today because we left very early in the morning."

"This means that you are not kept here in Vác?"

"No, I don't live here."

"Then, where is your permanent residence?"

The Cardinal asked the guard if he could answer this question. The answer was "No."

"Joseph, don't you need some warm clothes? I brought you some."

The Cardinal answered that he had everything he needed and his room was not cold.

"How do you spend your days, Joseph? What do you do all day long?"

From the Cardinal's answer, it was clear that his schedule had not fundamentally changed since July: he meditated, said Mass, read his Bible and his breviary, recited the Rosary, and took short afternoon walks.

"Can you sleep?"

"There are nights when I sleep well, but there are also other nights when I sleep very little."

The Cardinal then asked his mother about the family. He wanted to know how his sisters and their children and grandchildren were getting along. At the end of the visit, he gave his mother good wishes for her approaching feast day and said he was saying a novena for her. (Mother Mindszenty's patron saint, of course, was St. Barbara, whose feast day is December 4.)

The last thing the Cardinal said to his mother was this: "Mother, please go to Esztergom, or if you cannot go there yourself, then write Vicar General Beresztóczy and ask him to obtain a permit to come to see me before Christmas." (The Cardinal must have been told about Beresztóczy's election as Vicar, but not about his collaboration with the Communists in the Priests' Peace Movement, or about the Pope's appointment of Bishop Hamvas as Administrator of the Esztergom Archdiocese.)

Mother Mindszenty was well aware of the duplicitous role played by Beresztóczy as a "peace priest." She hesitated a moment. Then looking earnestly at her son so he could understand the hidden meaning of her guarded words, she answered in a serious tone: "You know, Joseph, I very much dislike mixing in Church politics. I really do not want to do what you ask, because one never knows what kind of a mistake one might make."

The Cardinal replied: "I must trust your judgment as to whether to inform the Vicar General or not." This answer showed that he understood his mother's warning that the Communists planned to mislead him by offering him the "favor" of a visit from Beresztóczy.

There is no doubt that the Communists wanted to use a meeting between Cardinal Mindszenty and Beresztóczy to promote their Peace Movement. After such a visit, Beresztóczy would have been ordered to make statements, allegedly from the Cardinal, advocating the Priests' Peace Movement. An invitation to Beresztóczy extended through the Cardinal's mother would have cleverly concealed the hidden hand of the Communists. Their shameless plotting failed because of Mother Mindszenty's quick and discerning reply.

The same afternoon I called on Archbishop Grősz to report on the morning visit. He was pleased to learn how Mother Mindszenty had foiled the Communists' maneuver.

CHAPTER 14

More Years in Prison

The way the Communists treated the Cardinal during the mock trial did not frighten Mother Mindszenty as much as her worry that they might kill him in prison and tell the world it was a "natural death." After her observations from her September 25, 1949 visit, she never could put that nagging thought out of her mind. Every time she saw him after that, she always asked him detailed questions about his health. In all her letters written to friends during this period, she went on and on about her son's physical condition. After seeing him on November 30, 1950 she wrote her New York friend on December 3: "Thank God, my son feels all right and seems to be well. Not having to worry about his health is my only consolation."

She used every chance she could to see the Cardinal. Before all the great Church feasts, especially Christmas, and the Cardinal's own special feast days, she literally stormed the Ministry of Justice with requests and letters. She begged that she be allowed to send the Cardinal a food package. In mid-December 1950, Sister Adelaide went to Budapest with a carefully-prepared Christmas parcel for the Cardinal. She delivered it to the Ministry of Justice and won a promise that it would be given to the Cardinal.

Mother Mindszenty felt that it was most unjust to allow prisoners to be visited only once every six months. She became convinced that the prison regulation was changed primarily to prevent her from seeing the Cardinal more often and keeping track of his physical condition. She often remarked: "Six months is such a long time; in that period, even a free man could die."

She was not content to wait out the six-month period in silence, but renewed her request every three months. In mid-February 1951, she sent a special request to see the Cardinal on March 19, the feast of St. Joseph. We all agreed that the best plan was for Sister Adelaide to take the petition to Budapest and get Dr. Farkas to deliver it personally to the Under Secretary in the Ministry of Justice, Stephen Timár.

Sister Adelaide made a night trip to the capital and went straight to Dr. Farkas' office. On his locked office door, she found a notice asking his clients to take their cases to another lawyer near by. Sister Adelaide was tired from her all-night trip, but dutifully delivered the letter, along with a cover letter from me, to the other lawyer. Later in the day, she learned that Dr. Farkas had been arrested during the night. She then returned to Szombathely to get other letters which she eventually personally delivered to John Pesti, the official in charge of prisons.

To our surprise, Pesti gave permission for Mother Mindszenty to visit her son on March 17. On March 16, I took her to Budapest by train and we again stayed at the Central Major Seminary. The next day, Mother Mindszenty and Sister Adelaide went at the appointed time to the prison on Markó Street, and from there Mother Mindszenty was driven to Vác. She saw the Cardinal, as before, in the prison reception room on the third floor. There was nothing unusual about this visit. They talked about family, friends, the trip to Budapest, and quite a bit about the Cardinal's health. Mother Mindszenty came away reassured that he was well. She said that he had lost weight, but she convinced herself it was the result of his voluntary fasting during Lent.

In her letter to the Ministry of Justice, she had also asked that the Cardinal have a priest for an Easter confession. This request was granted, and Father Béla Witz, Vicar of Budapest, was taken to Vác the same day. Since his office was in the Central Seminary where we were staying, I saw him on his return from the prison. To my inquiries he replied: "I found the Primate in good health and spirits."

That afternoon, many of our friends came to see us at the Seminary, but Dr. Farkas was conspicuous by his absence. No one seemed to know why he had been arrested. A pastor, Father Paul Bozsik, was arrested at the same time, so we suspected that the Government was preparing another anti-religious trial.

Two months later, Archbishop Grősz of Kalocsa was arrested. By May 15, 1951 it was obvious that Dr. Farkas would be a principal prosecution witness against the Archbishop. Dr. Farkas was a lifetime friend of the Archbishop and his diocesan legal adviser. In their younger days, they had studied theology together at the Pazmaneum in Vienna. Before ordination, Andrew Farkas opted for a legal career instead of the priesthood. His previous training in theology made him one of the foremost canon lawyers in Hungary.

The Communists needed to discredit Archbishop Grősz in order to break the resistance of the clergy against the Priests' Peace Movement. He was imprisoned for 38 days before arraignment, during which time he was subjected to the same brainwashing techniques which had been used on Cardinal Mindszenty. Archbishop Grősz's "trial," which lasted from June 22 to 28, was a carbon copy of the Cardinal's. In a half-conscious state, Archbishop Grősz publicly confessed that he was "a warmonger," had "committed high treason," was "a spy," and had "dealt illegally in foreign currencies." All 16 other defendants recited similar confessions against themselves. Dr. Farkas, brilliant lawyer though he was, was brainwashed into confessing that he had used his influence to persuade Archbishop Grősz to commit these "horrendous crimes." Archbishop Grősz, as chief defendant, received a 15-year sentence, and Dr. Farkas was sentenced to an even longer prison term.

After Archbishop Grősz was arrested, the Communists on May 21, 1951 introduced a bill in the Parliament to establish a National Bureau for Church Affairs. It read as follows: "A National Bureau for Church Affairs is hereby established to manage affairs between the Government and the different churches, to execute agreements with them, and to administer any subsidies given them." A "progressive Catholic" member of Parliament introduced the bill, declaring that the Bureau was set up in the best interests of the Church. He argued that, after the separation of Church and State in capitalist countries, the Church was abandoned by the State; but, in the "people's democracies," the Church was supported by the Government even after separation of Church and State.

The trial of Archbishop Grősz was still going on when personnel of the newly-established Bureau appeared with police escorts in the episcopal sees of Szeged, Vác, Székesfehérvár, and Veszprém. The police put these four bishops under house arrest and kept their residences surrounded. The bishops were "invited" to appoint priests from the Peace Movement to the key diocesan posts of vicar general and chancellor. At first, they all refused to be intimidated. After a few days, however, the news spread that Bishop Andrew Hamvas of Csanád, whom the Vatican had appointed Administrator of Esztergom, had reappointed Nicholas Beresztóczy as Vicar General of Esztergom, and had appointed another Peace Movement priest, Father Anthony Szécsy, as Vicar General of Csanád.

The other bishops still did not comply with the Communist orders and, therefore, were kept under house arrest in order to prevent their attending the next meeting of the Bishops' Conference which was held July 3, 1951 under the chairmanship of Archbishop Julius Czapik, who had succeeded to this office after Archbishop Grősz was arrested.

Archbishop Czapik adopted the policy that compromises had to be made to salvage whatever was possible. This attitude enabled the Communists to put the entire Catholic Church under their yoke in a short time. He took the position that Church officials should themselves dissolve all Catholic institutions which the Communists would not tolerate, including the seminaries, the preparatory seminaries, and a few still-surviving organizations. Archbishop Czapik dutifully issued any statements the Government demanded of him in order to publicly show his collaboration with the State, and then he persuaded the Bishops to accept these declarations.

At the July 3 meeting, he persuaded all the members of the Bishops' Conference (except the three absentees, Bishops

Badalik, Shvoy and Pétery) to sign a document in which they condemned "those Church officials whose subversive activities have just come to light."[1] Though no names were mentioned, this was widely interpreted as giving backhanded approval to the Government's action in arresting Archbishop Grősz and other clergy.

During the summer, "peace priests" took over the offices of vicar general and chancellor in every diocese. In addition, a representative of the National Bureau for Church Affairs sat in every episcopal residence, and kept the seal of the diocese as well as the key to the treasury and the archives. He monitored all incoming and outgoing mail. Without his permission, no one could see the bishop. He exercised a veto power over the bishop's every decision and over every meeting in the diocese.

These National Bureau officials saw to it that "peace priests" were assigned to the largest and best parishes and became district deans. These Government bureaucrats controlled all clerical activities, and harassed the best and most efficient priests. The Communist bureaucrats would give each bishop a list of so-called "reactionary" or "anti-democratic" priests and require the bishop to transfer them as "punishment," suspend them, or dismiss them from diocesan service.

The National Bureau for Church Affairs determined which priests could receive a salary and which were permitted to teach Christian doctrine. The prerequisite for either was to join the Peace Movement. In some parishes, where the laity caught on to these Communist tactics, they asked their pastor to make an external show of collaboration in order to prevent their parish from falling into the hands of an active "peace priest." When the National Bureau for Church Affairs finally forced the entire administration of the Church into the hands of the "peace priests," the spiritual discipline of the Church broke down completely.

The "peace priests" always subordinated the interests of the Church to those of the Government. They regularly issued "pastoral" letters exhorting the faithful to perform their "religious" duties more energetically — that is, to increase harvest yields and industrial production. For example, the Bureau for

Church Affairs required Bishop Paul Brezanóczy to issue the following pastoral letter on the first anniversary of the "Agreement":

"One of the essentials of the Agreement is that the Church must support Government policies. A spirit of mutual understanding and cooperation should permeate our pastoral activities. . . . Our general attitude must dispel any suspicion that our activities are not in harmony with the terms of the Agreement. Pastors must collaborate with the Government not only by the voluntary pledge of our services and properties, but also by using our priestly influence to exhort our parishioners to do likewise. It is our duty to convince ourselves of this, and then to convince others."[2]

The clergy doing pastoral work could satisfy the instructions set forth in such letters drafted by the National Bureau for Church Affairs only by sacrificing their priestly mission. Many refused this so-called "cooperation," labeling it injurious to the souls under their care. The Bureau for Church Affairs ordered Catholic officials to bring these recalcitrant priests to account and punish them. For example, a later pastoral letter which the Bureau required Bishop Brezanóczy to send to his clergy contained the following threats:

"It is with sincere regret that I am obliged to say that many of our priests did not take my previous instructions to heart. Ordinarily, it would be my duty to rebuke these wayward priests by name in this pastoral letter. I am refraining from doing this in order to give them a chance to make up for their neglect of duties. I have received complaints from several parts of our diocese, and therefore call the attention of my brother-priests to their obligation, by the end of this month, to notify me that they have conformed their activities to the instructions given in my pastoral letter."[3]

Without going into further description of the painful plight of the Church, we can sum up the situation by recording that the National Bureau for Church Affairs enslaved the Catholic Church and transformed it into a vehicle of total Communist control over the minds and morals of men. There is no similarity whatsoever between what happened in Hungary and the historical examples of Gallicanism, or Josephinism, or the

Caesaropapism fostered by the Czars. The essential difference
between those former examples of ecclesiastical subordina-
tion and the total enslavement of the Church in Hungary is
that the former, at least partially, tried to serve God and
religion, whereas the Communist objective is to stamp out all
belief in God. Under the Lenin dialectic, the Communists find
it wholly consistent to *use* the Church in order to *destroy*
religion.

Mother Mindszenty was deeply pained by the enslavement of the Church and the spiritual harm to Hungarians.
She was personally affected by the arrest of Archbishop Grősz.
When she heard about the inhuman treatment he had to
endure, she relived all the lying accusations the Cardinal had
to face during his imprisonment and mock trial. Her worry
about the Cardinal in prison was aggravated, and she pressed
for another permit to visit the Primate.

In May 1951 she asked me to take another request to
Budapest. I arrived in the capital just before Archbishop Grősz'
trial began. After the brutal interrogations which marked the
first day of his mock trial, I headed back to Szombathely.
Being completely worn out, I stopped overnight at the home
of a friend in one of the resorts on Lake Balaton. Hardly had
I set foot in his house when the president of the local soviet
arrived and ordered me to leave on the next train. He explained that he had received orders to expel every suspicious
stranger from the resort.

Meanwhile, Mother Mindszenty had sent other requests
and telegrams to Under Secretary Stephen Timár; but she
never received an answer. She poured out her dismay in two
letters to friends, the first one written on July 22, 1951:

"I have fallen behind in my letters. This was not because
of negligence, but because I have been busy sending many
requests to the Ministry for permission to visit my son. Even

by their own regulations, it is time for a visit and they should let me see him. But so far I have received no answer. I have already mailed a third request, but I suppose this will be useless. I do not even know where he is."

The second letter is dated August 16, 1951:

"In my last letter I wrote that I have not been permitted to visit my son. Now I must tell you that I even sent a telegram, but have received no reply. I am at a loss to know what to do. I am distraught, and simply can't understand their lack of sympathy. I would give a great deal to be able to write you a cheerful letter, but I am afraid I shan't live to see that day, as I am approaching 80. I am grateful to Our Lord Jesus for giving me these extra years. I have been able to bear all this sorrow only because of the many prayers said by so many kind friends."

After many requests and the pleadings of her friends, she finally received permission to visit the Cardinal on October 6, 1951. She was again driven to the prison at Vác where she and the Cardinal talked about their usual topics. She told him about the family's difficult financial situation, and how the Government bureaucrats were harassing the independent farmers to join the collective farm system. The Cardinal listened sympathetically to the news of his people's suffering and showed intense concern for their fate. Later, when Mother Mindszenty told me about her visit, she said:

"I am sorry I caused him so much worry. It occurred to me after I left that he knows only too well what is happening in our country under the Communists. Even as a young priest, he knew all about the Communists and their tactics. During the first Communist regime in 1919, he told the people in his speeches in Mindszent: 'Remember, if power remains in the hands of the Communists, even your scythe and spade will be stamped: *Government property!*'"

She reported that the Cardinal appeared to be in good health. She had broached her question this way: "Joseph, haven't you been to Mátra or one of the other health resorts?" Actually, she was just probing to find out if there were any truth to the Government-spread rumors that, because of the Cardinal's serious illness, he had received special medical treatment and rest at a Hungarian resort. The Cardinal just smiled and answered, "Dear Mother, health resorts are not for prisoners."

In the Veszprém Seminary, a theology student put a notice on the bulletin board on February 9, 1952 asking that the anniversary of the Cardinal's trial be commemorated by special prayers. The local official of the National Bureau for Church Affairs then declared that this incident provided ample evidence of "institutional guilt." He took this offense before the Council of Ministers which decreed that the Veszprém Seminary be closed and its professors prohibited from serving as priests any longer.

Three years later, we discovered that the "theological student" who had posted the notice had been collaborating with the secret police from the very beginning.

After the Veszprém Seminary was closed, representatives of the few remaining theological academies and seminaries went to Budapest for a meeting chaired by Archbishop Czapik. Beresztóczy, the Peace Movement chairman, was present and ominously warned the professors that they must give their students an "up-to-date" education. He said that certain additional seminaries would also be closed, including the Szombathely Seminary of which I was then the Prefect as well as a teaching professor. Soon after this meeting, I received confidential information that the Vicar General of our diocese (who had been appointed by the National Bureau for Church Affairs) had said that he planned to dismiss me at the end of the school year.

I had suffered from stomach and gall bladder ailments ever since the Russian occupation began. Since ordinary medical treatment had not cured me, I had asked the leading surgeon at our local hospital on several occasions over the previous seven years whether surgery might help. He had always refused to operate, being convinced that surgery would not help under conditions of such emotional strain. At my last checkup, I told him that the Seminary would be dissolved at the end of the school year and I would be dismissed. As my physician, he advised me to leave the country.

Szombathely was only about 16 miles from the border, but it was guarded with barbed wire, mined fields, and Soviet police. Of course, the Government would not issue passports to leave the country. One of my friends located a trusted guide who helped me on the night of April 30, 1952, at the risk of our lives, to cross the Iron Curtain to freedom.

Two weeks before, on April 16, 1952, I accompanied Mother Mindszenty to Budapest for the last time. She had arrived in Szombathely on the morning train and was suffering from a severe cold. Monsignor Géfin and I persuaded her to take a plane to Budapest, rather than the train. She was afraid of flying, so we had some difficulty convincing her. We told her that it was unwise for a sick person to make a 10-hour train journey. She could go by air in an hour and be rested for the next day's visit.

We bought our tickets and went to the airport in the afternoon. As we boarded the plane, she said, "You have flown several times before, haven't you?" "No," I answered, "this is my first flight." "That's quite interesting," she remarked. "You and the good Rector recommended the plane so highly that I had the impression you both were experienced flyers."

This little colloquy seemed to take the edge off her nervousness. By the time we got to Budapest, she was glad we had talked her out of the tiresome train ride.

The next day, she again visited the Cardinal in the Vác prison. When she returned to the Seminary, she told us the Cardinal was in a happy mood and good physical condition. This letter to a friend in New York on April 22 reflects her cheerful frame of mind:

"Finally I can write and share my joy. I saw Joseph after Easter, on April 17. He is very thin but in good health, thank God. He was glad to see me and said: 'Dear Mother, it has been a long time since you last came.' I told him, 'Joseph, that is only because I have not been allowed to see you. I would come often if only I were permitted!'"

We stayed two days in Budapest, and then I accompanied her back to Mindszent. This was the last time I saw her. We communicated with each other after that by letters and messages we could occasionally get across the Iron Curtain. In these rare messages, she continued to tell me about her visits to the prison.

Mother Mindszenty saw the Cardinal in October 1952, in the spring of 1953, and again in the fall of 1953. When she wrote me about these visits, she stressed each time that his health was good. When she visited him on Easter of 1954, however, she was surprised and pained to find him in a pitiful condition. In her letter to me after that visit, she said:

"I found my son in a very bad way. He is quite thin and appears almost black from starvation. I was shocked to see him. I asked him, 'Joseph, is this how you are treated by the Government? Why do I find you like this after we have given the Government so much of our produce that practically none is left for us at home?'

"Two guards were present and must have heard what I said. When they moved out of hearing for a moment, I asked my son, 'Joseph, it wasn't very prudent of me to say that, was it?' He replied, 'I'm glad you said it!'

"I earnestly begged the prison officials to let me mail him a food parcel each month so that he would be better fed. But they would not permit it. Later on, a messenger informed me that no parcels would be allowed, but that I could send him money. I told him I did not have any money, but could easily send him food. I finally scraped together 100 forints to send."

Mother Mindszenty wrote me again later that summer:

"At last I have succeeded in getting permission to see Joseph every three months! Remember in the spring I found him in such poor health, and complained to the officials about the way they had mistreated him? Apparently, they became ashamed. Perhaps this is why I got permission. Now I have found him somewhat improved."

At the end of October 1954, she wrote me:

"On October 26, I went to see my dear son. This was the third time since Easter. He is much better now than he was. Since August I have mailed him 300 forints for food, as money is the only thing they will let me send. They will let me bring food only when I visit him."

Knowing that all mail going outside the country was censored by the secret police, she wrote very cautiously. Therefore, it was only when I saw the Cardinal on November 1, 1956, after his liberation, that I was able to question him and find out how seriously ill he was during those years of his imprisonment.

The Cardinal told me, "Twice I was near death." He said he had tuberculosis during the winter of 1954. Stricken with a terrible fever, he lost weight rapidly and dwindled to 90 pounds, about half his regular weight. He received neither medical care nor decent food. In spite of prison regulations which supposedly required prompt treatment for serious illnesses, he was left in a dark and unhealthy prison cell.

Undoubtedly the Communists considered this a good opportunity to accomplish what we all dreaded: a "natural end" to the Cardinal's life. He discovered their diabolical intent one day when the prison doctor "inadvertently" let the Cardinal catch a glimpse of his medical file which diagnosed his case as hopeless and revealed that the prison authorities planned on doing nothing at all to save him.

The Cardinal summoned all his physical and spiritual strength and prayed that God not permit him to die while in the hands of the Bolsheviks. After a few days, he was transferred to a prison hospital. The Communists evidently intended that, when he died, it would appear that prison medical regulations were being observed. In the hospital, he was put in a clean, sunny room, and the chief physician, Dr. László Szabó, did everything he could to care for the Cardinal. The improved atmosphere, medical treatment, adequate food, and the Cardinal's determination to live, all contributed to his recovery.

The Cardinal became very ill again in the early summer of 1955, and no treatment seemed to halt the progressive deterioration in his health. Dr. Szabó, believing that the Cardinal's death was imminent, asked the Government officials to move him away from the hospital, as he did not want the Primate to die under his supervision.

This was the Cardinal's condition as the four great powers prepared to attend the Geneva Conference on July 17, 1955. Suddenly, on July 16, Radio Budapest broadcast the news that the Government had suspended the Cardinal's life sentence and placed him under house arrest because of his age, his illness, and the request of the Bishops' Conference.

Cardinal Mindszenty was taken to Püspökszentlászló in southern Hungary, the former summer residence of the Bishops of Pécs, where he was guarded by 16 agents of the secret police. The clean air, the beautiful landscape, and the abundant woods and flowers had a dramatic effect on the Cardinal's body, enervated as it was by years in a dark prison cell in the damp and depressing stone world underneath Budapest.

He was visited daily in his third-floor room by a young doctor from Pécs, proud of the fact that he could show his ability by curing the Cardinal. The doctor was a convinced Marxist and often boasted to the Cardinal that he would regain his health not by God's help, but through the physician's medical knowledge. By the time the Cardinal had been out of prison a year, he was a healthy man — no doubt due to a combination of Divine Providence and the Cardinal's will to recover, as well as the physician's skill.

His mother was allowed to see him in Püspökszentlászló

on July 26. She happily wrote me that the Cardinal's health had improved dramatically:

"I found my son fairly well in spite of his great loss of weight. He is cheerful and has a hearty appetite. We were together most of the time I was there. At last we could talk about family affairs without interruption. He asked me if people were saying he had asked for the transfer from the prison. 'Yes, it was quite a sensation,' I told him. 'But it is not true that I requested it,' he said.

"After lunch he called me: 'Come, Mother, I want to show you something.' In the bedroom, on the window sill, were a couple of cookies and apples I had taken him in May. 'But surely they aren't any good now,' I told him. 'They're still good to remind me of your love,' he replied.

"He asked me about the Bishops and the priests. I told him all I knew. I told him they could not act as they wanted to. He said, 'Mother, I have no hard feelings about those who worked against me.' I do admire his charity.

"He told me that a doctor comes to see him every day and that a blood sample had been taken the day before. He seems physically and mentally healthy. As he has good food now, he is bound to regain his strength.

"His residence is in an excellent location. The entire area is enclosed by a wooden fence and surrounded by many trees, especially fir trees. On the porch there is a table and chair where a guard sits all the time. Otherwise, my son is free to walk about the grounds."

On October 14, 1955, Archbishop Grősz was also taken to Püspökszentlászló. On November 2, before winter set in, both were transferred to the well-known Almássy manor in Felsőpetény in Nógrád County. There they were also kept under guard by 16 secret police agents. On February 25, 1956, Archbishop Grősz was transferred to Tószeg in Szolnok County.

Cardinal Mindszenty remained alone in Felsőpetény. In these 15 months of house arrest, his mother was able to visit him only four times: twice in Püspökszentlászló and twice in Felsőpetény. On these occasions, they were left alone for a while by the secret police.

The Cardinal's Residence in Budapest on October 31, 1956. This is the tank which brought Cardinal Mindszenty from Felsőpetény.

CHAPTER 15

Those Few Days of Freedom

Some of the most dramatic and amazing events of the 20th century took place during the last several days of October and the first several days of November 1956. My eyewitness account is recorded in this letter which I wrote to Mother Mindszenty.

Budapest
November 2, 1956

Dear Mother Barbara:

It is with the greatest joy that I tell you I am home in Budapest and writing you on behalf of the Cardinal!

In a previous letter, I told you that I moved from Germany to Austria for the summer in order to work with the Diocesan Printing Press in St. Pölten to publish three volumes of a collection of documents dealing with Cardinal Mindszenty. This will be a scholarly compilation of the Cardinal's pastoral letters, speeches and other important statements, printed in both Hungarian and German. While in Vienna during the last few months, I could watch how the Communist regime in Hungary has been shaken to its foundations.

When I first heard about the Revolution, I was not only surprised but skeptical. On October 25, curiosity and excitement led me to the Austro-Hungarian border. It was noon when I reached the customs house at Hegyeshalom. I could hardly believe my eyes! The barricade was down, the Red Star on the soldiers' caps had been replaced by the Hungarian tricolor, and traffic was proceeding normally.

Watching from the Austrian side, I saw an army truck approach. A doctor and four soldiers got out. They had come from Budapest and wanted to take medicines and food back to the wounded. I crossed the border to join them, and then led them back to the Austrian side where tents and supplies had been set up by the Red Cross and by International

Catholic Charities. We talked while I helped them load their truck. They confirmed the unbelievable — that in Budapest and the larger Hungarian cities, workers and students were actually fighting Government troops and Soviet Army units!

Representatives of all the European countries were clustered at the border. There were swarms of reporters from newspapers, radio networks and wire services, all excitedly and sympathetically talking about the great news. I spoke with the leaders of the various charitable organizations, on whose instructions the next day we helped load trucks with enormous quantities of food, clothing, bandages, and medicines.

With several Hungarian friends, I stayed at the border to help organize voluntary service units. We prepared all kinds of supplies and we loaded trucks leaving for the interior of the country. We forwarded the requests from Budapest to Austrian, Belgian, German and other welfare organizations. We gave the press all the military and political news which came out of Budapest. We worked day and night without sleep or rest, oscillating between hope and despair. We were so excited we could not possibly try to sleep.

In the midst of such feverish activity on the afternoon of October 30, I heard the news that, on the threshold of victory, the newly-formed revolutionary Government had called Cardinal Mindszenty to the capital. I was apprehensive about this, fearing that His Eminence was still in Communist hands and that this call might be used as a pretext for deporting him to Siberia. I worried about this all evening.

After midnight, Radio Vienna broadcast the wonderful news that Hungarian revolutionary troops had liberated the Cardinal from the hands of the secret police! He was on his way to Budapest and great crowds were gathering to welcome him along the way.

After daylight came and I verified these reports, I decided to leave immediately for Budapest in spite of the danger. With the help of friends from Győr, I arrived here in Budapest at the Primate's residence yesterday at noon.

From the moment His Eminence set foot here, there has been a tremendous crowd in and around the house. There is no end to the people who come to see him, not only from Budapest but from every part of Hungary. The whole street adjoining the residence is filled with visitors. The rooms, the courtyard, the corridors and the stairways are overflowing with people who want to see him.

The Cardinal uses the two rooms off the central staircase and receives visitors in the two rooms directly opposite. When I arrived at the residence, I just couldn't wait in that long line, but tried to thread my way straight to the Cardinal's reception room. As I reached the door, reporters from an American radio network were being ushered into the reception room. I quickly joined their group and entered with them.

The Cardinal spotted me immediately. Before I could even greet him, he said, "Thank you so much for the many services you have rendered my mother." Not knowing exactly what to say, I blurted out that I had come from Vienna. "I know everything," he replied.

I realized that you had told the Cardinal about how I had worked so hard to help you get permission to see him in prison. I am glad you told him. During dinner, I gave the Cardinal the details of several events from those bygone years. He was especially thrilled by my account of the dedication of the statue of the Sacred Heart in Mindszent, and he enjoyed the humorous side of our plane trip in 1952.

After my arrival yesterday, the Cardinal asked me to stay with him and help him receive foreign visitors. He held audiences all day yesterday until 5:30 P.M. He received Minister of State Zoltán Tildy and Deputy Minister of Defense Paul Maléter, representing the new free Hungarian Government.

Another Government representative that afternoon told the Cardinal all the details of the negotiations with the Russians. The Russians promised to leave Hungary, gave their consent to free elections, and stated they did not object to Hungary's neutrality. The Cardinal advised the Government not to believe these Communist statements, but to plead its own cause immediately at the United Nations. That these Soviet promises were also discounted by other Hungarians is indicated by a remark made by one of Tildy's representatives:

An inside view of the Cardinal's Residence in Budapest, 1956. The Cardinal could never afford to have it repaired after the destruction of World War II.

"The Soviets are barbarians without consciences, and therefore we cannot trust their promises."

Dear Mother Barbara, as you can see, the situation is still quite dangerous. His Eminence has asked me to tell you everything in this letter. The real reason I am writing you in such detail about the political situation is to dissuade you from any thought of traveling to either Budapest or Esztergom. Please wait until the political and military situation is clarified, and do not come here until His Eminence sends you a message that it would be safe. Please wait for a personal message from the Cardinal which Sister Adelaide will bring you.

At this moment, the people in Budapest are filled with joy. The whole Free World is thrilled about the Cardinal's liberation. He received at least 2,000 congratulatory telegrams here yesterday. At noon yesterday a telegram in Latin arrived from Pope Pius XII. Here is a translation:

"Eight years ago, our paternal heart was grieved by your illegal removal from your Archbishop's See, an action which we vigorously protested many times, especially during a public consistory. The news of your liberation fills our soul with happiness. At this moment, there is great joy not only in your own nation, but in the entire Catholic world.

"With a grateful heart, we give thanks to the Lord that He has deigned to listen to the continuing supplications of the faithful, and that His grace has shone brightly on your faith and fortitude, so sorely tried by the sufferings you willingly accepted for Christ's sake. May this be a sign from Heaven that the Hungarian nation will be blest and that you and your fellow Bishops may be able to renew your apostolic works.

"Our heartfelt wish is that the Catholic faith, so tested by errors and bloodshed, may be renewed again, and that the fidelity of the Hungarian people to the Church and to the Holy See — so wondrously inherited from your ancestors — may receive new strength for the future.

"At this moment when we ask God's eternal rest for the victims of the recent tragic events, we send you, our beloved son who has always been present in our thoughts and prayers, as a token of divine assistance, our abundant love and apostolic blessing, extending it also to all the Bishops, priests and faithful who have been the victims of the current tribulation.

"Pope Pius XII"

Many touching episodes happened here yesterday. Before lunch I went down to the kitchen to see what was going on. I found the storeroom completely empty. Mrs. Bodor, who is in charge of the kitchen, said that the only meat in the house this week was a duck which she had cooked for the Cardinal's arrival. I immediately phoned Catholic Charities in Vienna and asked for some food at the Archbishop's residence.

In the afternoon, a small truck arrived loaded with food, a gift to the Cardinal from the bakers of Vienna. The three-man crew which brought it begged me to take them in to see him. When His Eminence thanked them for their "charity," one of them answered:

"Your Eminence, we did not bring you charity. We simply want to pay back the Hungarians in material goods for all they have given the world spiritually."

"It is a pity," Mrs. Bodor said later, "that we couldn't keep the food here in this house where we need it. His Eminence gave it all away to charitable organizations."

After all his appointments and audiences yesterday, I had the chance to visit with the Cardinal alone. I know you will be most interested in knowing the details of how he was liberated from the hands of the secret police on the afternoon of October 30.

The Cardinal had heard on the radio on October 23 about the student demonstrations. The next day, his secret-police guards confiscated his radio and refused to let him see any more newspapers. From these actions and the guards' nervous behavior, he concluded that the demonstrations had had a considerable effect. But he did not dare suppose that Freedom Fighters were actually battling for their liberty in Budapest and in other key cities. He spent the whole week in prayer, asking the Virgin Mary to intercede for Hungary in its hour of greatest crisis.

His guards were solemn and tight-lipped all week and did not disclose one word about the revolutionary events. The chief of the guards finally came to the Cardinal and told him to get ready, as his life was in danger and they had to leave the place.

"But who endangers my life here?" the Cardinal asked. "The mob," the chief guard answered bitterly.

"I am not afraid of the people," the Cardinal said, "and I do not intend to leave this house."

The chief policeman then left, but soon returned with two others and demanded: "Will you come with us if we make a show of force?"

"I will not leave this house," the Cardinal replied with determination, "and I will not submit to violence."

Of course he had no real hope of preventing his removal by force, but he bravely challenged them on the chance that the guards might be acting on impulse without orders from higher up. He also considered the possibility that they might be planning to hand him over to the Russians.

The secret police were preparing to take him forcibly when suddenly another guard rushed in. He announced that a Russian army truck had just pulled up in front of the house. Everyone ran to the window to see who was in it.

John Horváth, the chief of the National Bureau for Church Affairs, jumped out of the truck, barged in to see the Cardinal, and demanded that he leave the house and go immediately with the police. The Cardinal told Horváth that he would not leave the house for any reason and vigorously protested this irresponsible and illegal order.

Horváth became very excited and apprehensive. He began using violent language and threatened to use force to evict the Cardinal. But an unexpected turn of events prevented this.

Peasants in the neighborhood around the Almássy manor had become alarmed by the appearance of the Russian army truck in front of the house where they knew the Cardinal was kept. They armed themselves with hoes, scythes, pitchforks and other farm implements and gathered to save the Cardinal. While Horváth was arguing inside, the peasants surrounded the house and began shouting demands that the Cardinal be released. When Horváth heard their angry clamor, and saw through the window that a large crowd had surrounded the house, he stormed back to the army truck and drove out of Felsőpetény as fast as he could.

When this happened, the chief of the secret-police guards lost all his nerve, and from then on was only concerned about saving his own skin. Meanwhile, the crowd outside continued clamoring for the Cardinal's freedom. The guards ran from window to window trying to quiet the demonstrators who paid no attention whatsoever, but shouted all the louder.

Finally, the frightened secret policemen went into a corner to assess their situation. When they came out of their huddle, they all came and stood politely in front of the Cardinal. The chief guard announced that he and his men had decided to join the Revolution and were going over to the side of the people. He concluded with, "Eminence, from this moment on, you are free!"

A few moments later, a unit of fighting troops arrived from the army camp in Rétság which was in the hands of the Freedom Fighters. They had heard about the Russian army truck bringing the head of the Bureau for Church Affairs to the Cardinal's house. They intercepted and captured Horváth on his way back to Budapest.

Meanwhile, free Hungarian telephone operators had succeeded in tapping the phone between the secret police at Almássy manor and Budapest. They picked up information which convinced the commander of the Freedom Fighters in Rétság, Major Pallavicini, that Cardinal Mindszenty was in

Cardinal Mindszenty with Major Pallavicini. The Cardinal is pictured here with the officer who headed the unit of Freedom Fighters which liberated him from Felsőpetény on October 30, 1956. Major Pallavicini was later captured by the Communists and executed in 1957.

danger of being deported to Siberia. Major Pallavicini quickly led a fighting unit to Felsőpetény to save the Cardinal.

The Cardinal greeted the Major, his soldiers, and the local peasants most cordially. He asked them to release the secret police and let them go free and unharmed, which was done after they were disarmed.

After the secret police had left, the free Hungarians searched the entire house. They found a large cache of grenades and machine guns in the basement, as well as plenty of ammunition.

The walls of the upper floors had all been bugged. That is how, dear Mother Barbara, they knew everything you and the Cardinal discussed during your visits there.

It was the consensus that the Cardinal should move to the army barracks in Rétság, and so at 10:05 P.M. they left Almássy manor.

After eight years of imprisonment, you can imagine how thrilled the Cardinal was to be freed by the Hungarian people he loves so much. He told me how much he enjoyed those first hours he spent with the soldiers in their barracks. "They were all so happy," he told me, "with high hopes for a better and brighter future."

After reaching the army barracks, they decided that the Cardinal should go to Budapest in the morning. He said to the soldiers, "But, my sons, what will guarantee that I will arrive safely in Budapest?"

"Only our lives," the Major answered. "Nothing but our lives," the soldiers repeated enthusiastically. The Cardinal told them: "My sons, I trust you. We will leave for Budapest in the morning."*

Early on October 31, the entourage left Rétság and headed for Budapest. The Cardinal rode in an army truck, accompanied by three tanks and a fourth with a formidable fixed turret. All along the route, the farmers and townspeople welcomed him with flowers. On his arrival at the Primate's residence at 8:55 A.M. Wednesday, he gave his blessing to the crowd from the balcony and then said Mass in the chapel.

*Major Pallavicini was later captured by the Communists and executed in 1957.

Cardinal Mindszenty with the Freedom Fighters who brought him to Budapest.
This picture was taken in front of his residence in Budapest, 1956.

I want to tell you how especially happy I am to give you firsthand knowledge of what you want to know most of all — that His Eminence is completely healthy and vigorous in both mind and body. Of course, his long imprisonment has taken its toll. But in spite of this, his working capacity is as great as ever. Here is what he said in a short radio message yesterday evening:

"After so many years in prison, I am once again able to speak to you, dear sons and daughters of Hungary. I do not bear a grudge against anyone. A magnificent heroism has liberated our country. Such a fight for freedom is without parallel in history. Our young men deserve every honor. I offer my gratitude and prayers for the glorious patriotism of our soldiers, our workers and our farmers.

"Our country's situation is very serious. We lack the political and economic conditions necessary to resume a normal life. It is urgent that we find a way to solve our critical problems. After a preliminary briefing, I will send the nation a message which I hope may contribute to a solution of our present crisis."

The Cardinal has called a meeting of the Bishops' Conference to make the most pressing decisions and to discuss the substance of his next radio message. Archbishop Grősz and Bishops Shvoy and Pétery have already indicated their eagerness to participate.

I am so sorry I cannot come to see you personally. I must return to Vienna, and from there I intend to go to Rome.

Respectfully yours,

Joseph Vecsey

CHAPTER 16

A Refugee in His Own Country

After discussing the Hungarian situation with several members of the Bishops' Conference, Cardinal Mindszenty addressed the nation by radio on the evening of November 3, 1956:

"Nowadays men often say they are going to turn over a new leaf and speak frankly. In my case, there is no need for a new leaf. With the help of Divine Providence, I am the same man I was before I was imprisoned. Though prison has taken its toll of my physical strength, I stand by my convictions with the same spirit and mind I had eight years ago. I have always spoken frankly and forthrightly, saying what I believe to be right and true, and I continue in plain-spoken language today. This is not a recording but a live broadcast so I can give my message personally to our nation and to the world.

"For the first time, I can publicly thank our friends in other lands for their precious help. First, I express my gratitude to His Holiness Pius XII who so often remembers the head of the Catholic Church in Hungary in his prayers. Then, I extend my deepest appreciation to those heads of Governments and Parliaments, to the leaders of various churches, and to many organizations and individuals for showing their concern and extending a helping hand to me and to my country during my years in prison. May God bless and reward them.

"I also want to thank the representatives of the world press and radio who have played such an indispensable role in reporting what happened in Hungary. I am glad to be able publicly to express my appreciation to them.

"Now I want to talk about our present crisis. Every civilized nation has sided with us and is trying to help. This is a great tribute to the moral force exerted throughout the world

Cardinal Mindszenty's radio message from Budapest on November 1, 1956.
This was his first message after being freed by the Hungarian Freedom
Fighters.

by one very small country. Hungary has one special distinction: in a thousand years of history, no nation has suffered more for freedom. After the reign of our first king, St. Stephen, we became a great power. After the victory of Belgrade 500 years ago, we had a population as large as England's. But again and again we had to fight for our survival and to man the ramparts of Western freedom. Because we spent so much of our energy defending Western civilization, our own ranks were thinned and our progress limited.

"This is the first time in our embattled history that Hungary has won the powerful sympathy and friendship of practically every nation. We are deeply touched, and every Hungarian is glad to see that our friends abroad are showing their love of freedom by their willingness to lend us a helping hand. This may be the plan of Divine Providence to make mankind more conscious of a oneness with other nations. Our national anthem echoes the same theme: 'Bless Hungarians, God on high; reach to them Thine arm of might.'

"Our national anthem also asks for help 'against our foes.' In our grim situation, we hope we have no foes, just as we are not the enemy of any nation. We want to live in friendship with every other country.

"In a nation such as Hungary, which has such a rich and varied history, we can reflect on the failures and successes of previous efforts to live at peace with other nations. Through various confrontations and crises, we can read the painful signs of progress.

"It is a mark of modern times to respect and seek progress in all things. Even old national feelings, therefore, must be reexamined and reevaluated. National aspirations and the spirit of patriotism should not be a constant source of conflict among nations, but should promote true peaceful cooperation based on justice.

"Patriotism, therefore, should thrive all the more in a world which respects a nation's legitimate values and culture. One nation's progress should help others to progress.

"It is one of nature's laws that physical survival requires people to depend on one another. This is also true in the life of nations. We Hungarians wish to serve as the standard-bearer of true peace in the European family of nations. We seek a genuine friendship with all of them, as well as with more distant countries. A small nation, we want to live in mutual friendship with the great United States, and with the powerful Russian Empire. We seek to be good neighbors to Prague, Bucharest, Warsaw and Belgrade. I must mention our particular gratitude to Austria because of her brotherly friendship during our present struggle. For this help, she is held in special esteem in the heart of every Hungarian.

"Our whole future depends on the attitude of the 200-million-strong Soviet Empire — and on the intentions of its army stationed within our boundaries. Radio broadcasts inform us that the Soviets are sending reinforcements to their units stationed in Hungary. We are neutral and have given the Russian Empire no provocation for bloodshed. We know that, in the past, the thought that we would esteem them far more if they did *not* enslave us, never entered the minds of the Soviet leaders.

"Only an enemy nation attacks another nation. We have not attacked Russia! We sincerely hope that Russian armed forces will soon be withdrawn from our country.

"Our internal situation is very critical. Because of our military and political crisis, production and work in the whole country have stopped. We are threatened by widespread starvation. A nation which is a mere bag of bones is fighting desperately for its freedom.

"Therefore, it is immediately incumbent on all of us to go to work, to resume production, and to tackle the task of reconstruction. This must be done without delay, in the interest of our local communities as well as the nation as a whole. Our national survival is at stake.

"In performing our duties, let us never forget that our struggle is a fight for freedom and not a revolution. After 1945, following an unsuccessful and, for us, a meaningless war, the Communist regime took power by force. The Hungarian people have branded the officials of that regime with every sign of contempt, hatred and aversion. That regime has been swept away by the people themselves. This is conclusively proved by the fact that the flower of our nation's youth

Cardinal Mindszenty's press interview on November 1, 1956. His first press interview after being freed took place in Budapest in front of the main entrance of his episcopal residence, which had been largely destroyed.

is today battling in the front lines of a life-and-death struggle for freedom.

"Our Hungarian people are fighting for freedom because they want to be free to decide their own destiny, to elect their own Government, and to keep for themselves the benefits of their own economic production. We will not allow the noble purpose of this effort to be diverted for any ulterior political motive or exploited for an illicit advantage.

"New elections, free from unfair advantage for any group, must be held. Each political party should have an equal chance. The elections should be carried out under international supervision. I will remain outside of all political parties and play no political role whatsoever because my office is removed from politics.

"However, as a pastor of souls, I must warn my compatriots that after the admirable spirit of unity displayed during the last hectic days of October, we must not give way to party strife and discord. Our nation needs many things, but not party bosses or greedy political factions. Politics must be secondary now; our first concern is our daily bread and the very survival of our nation.

"The brutalities committed by the officials of the overthrown regime reveal the need for future legal prosecutions in every part of the country. However, this must be carried out only by independent and impartial courts. We must not indulge in private acts of vengeance. Officials and functionaries of the former regime are certainly responsible for what they did, for what they failed to do, and for all their unjust actions. However, preoccupation with revenge and the hasty denunciation of others can only handicap the resumption of production and the economic recovery of our nation. Our primary task is to extricate our nation from its present perilous military and economic situation.

"I must stress the following obligations and duties: We live in a constitutional State, in a society without rigid social classes, with a national objective of developing democratic institutions grounded in the principle of private property fairly and justly regulated. We seek to become a country governed exclusively by those loyal to the principles of our own national culture. As the head of the Catholic Church in Hungary, I solemnly confirm — just as we made clear in a pastoral letter issued by the Bishops' Conference in 1945 — that we will aid legitimate and just progress. The Hungarian people want progress while still preserving all our valuable institutions which have such a glorious past.

"In my capacity as head of the Catholic Church in Hungary, I pledge that the 6½ million Catholics will assist in eliminating every trace of the former regime's violence and tyrannical impostures against the Church. Such action is the natural consequence of our attachment to our ancestral faith and morals, plus our devotion to the laws of the realm which are almost as old as the Church itself. This message to our nation does not pretend to be exhaustive, but I want to say enough to make my sentiments on these matters clear.

"Finally, I must pose this question. What are the supporters of the fallen regime thinking now? If their leaders had been adequately grounded in religion and morality, would they have had to flee when their actions were publicly exposed? This is only one of the reasons why the Church insists that freedom of religious education be resumed immediately. We also expect, in all justice, the restoration to the Church of Catholic institutions, societies and press.[1]

"From this moment on, we will stand guard to make sure that promises and performance go hand in hand. What can be done today, must not be left till tomorrow. We sincerely want to promote the welfare of the whole nation and we put our trust in Divine Providence."

This message broadcast by Cardinal Mindszenty on behalf of the Bishops' Conference made clear that the Church tried to solve all the pending problems between Church and State by good-faith negotiations. Unilateral ecclesiastical measures were taken only to reestablish discipline among the

clergy. For example, when the Bishops banned the Priests'
Peace Movement, this was properly in their own sphere of
episcopal authority, and an effort to terminate what the
Cardinal referred to as the former regime's "tyrannical
impostures."

At the same time, the Bishops declared they would not
oppose "democratic socialism" or a "classless society" or "agrarian reform." But, as the Cardinal declared in the name of all
the Bishops, the Church had a right to protect itself against
its own properties being confiscated and then used to sub-
sidize the Communist-collaborating priests of the Peace
Movement. The Church and all religious institutions should
certainly be free to spend their own money.

After his radio broadcast, Cardinal Mindszenty returned
to the Primate's residence in Budapest. On the morning of
November 4, he and millions of Hungarians heard Imre Nagy,
Prime Minister of the free Hungarian Government, personally
announce on the radio: "Soviet troops have attacked Budapest at dawn with the clear intention of overthrowing the free
democratic Hungarian Government. Our troops are fighting
the Soviets for right and freedom, and Government officials
remain at their posts."

As the day progressed, the last desperate cries of free
Hungary went out over teletype and radio. A series of teletype messages from the Budapest newspaper *Szabad Nép* to
the Associated Press included these appeals: "Please tell the
world of the treacherous attack against our struggle for liberty.
. . . Help! Help! Help! . . . S O S! S O S! S O S! . . . We
have almost no weapons — only light machine guns, Russian-
made long rifles and some carbines. We haven't any kind of
heavy guns. The people are jumping at the tanks and throwing in hand grenades. . . . The Hungarian people are not
afraid of death. It is only a pity that we can't stand for
long. . . .

"What is the United Nations doing? Give us a little en-
couragement. . . . We hope the U.N. meeting won't be too
late."

As the Russian tanks, MIG fighters, and overwhelming
superiority in weapons were crushing free Hungary, Zoltán

Mother Mindszenty
in Mindszent,
1958.

Cardinal
Mindszenty
at the
American
Legation
1958.

Tildy asked Cardinal Mindszenty to attend a Cabinet meeting in the Parliament house. Tildy's request is the reason why the Cardinal did not fall again into Communist hands that very night. While the Russian tanks lined up in front of the Parliament, the Cabinet members took refuge in the Yugoslav embassy. It had become completely impossible for the Cardinal to return to the Primate's residence, which was on the other side of the Danube.

Amidst the street turmoil and confusion, the Cardinal threaded his way past the rows of Russian tanks and took refuge at the nearby American legation. Once there, he had to wait about 15 minutes before being granted permission to stay. It took that long to obtain an answer from Washington, D.C. to the urgent request that the United States grant political asylum to the Hungarian Primate.

Three days later, the Cardinal sent this message from the American legation in Budapest to President Dwight Eisenhower: "Shipwrecked in the fight for Hungarian freedom, I have found a haven, thanks to your generosity. While a guest in your legation, I am at the same time a refugee in my own homeland. Your country's hospitality has saved me from certain death."[2]

Political asylum saved Cardinal Mindszenty from death, but not from another imprisonment lasting 15 years. Although no longer in a Communist jail, he was nevertheless truly a prisoner. He could watch the tribulations of his people and the persecution of the Church only through small fourth-floor windows. He was not allowed to send or receive mail. He was not allowed to receive visitors or to have any contacts with Hungarians. During all those years, the Communist secret police kept watch outside around the clock to arrest and reimprison him if he left the building.

While the Cardinal was in the American legation, his

Cardinal Mindszenty and his Mother. This rare picture was taken at the American Legation in 1959.

mother could visit him only when the Communist Government permitted it. The first time this happened was on Christmas 1956. After that, the Government gave permission only twice a year. She visited the Cardinal a total of only six more times.

Mother Mindszenty died on February 5, 1960 at the age of 85. Her health failed only during the last few weeks. She began to complain that her memory was failing and that she got sleepy while saying her prayers. She kept working until the very last day. She died at her home, in peace with the Lord, surrounded by her large family.

In his book *The Mother*, Cardinal Mindszenty refers to a remark in Victor Hugo's poem, *Exile*, that it is a heartbreaking sorrow to be "prevented from hurrying to the grave of a mother." This was one more sacrifice the Cardinal had to make. The Communist Government would not permit him to attend his mother's funeral. He sent a beautiful wreath which was placed on her grave by a Catholic member of the staff at the French legation in Budapest.

After President John F. Kennedy met Nikita Khrushchev in Vienna in June 1961, it became very noticeable that various groups were busily trying to induce the Cardinal to leave Hungary. They engaged in various diplomatic intrigues and spread their false propaganda throughout the world press. Periodically, with almost push-button precision, a global propaganda machine churned out fabricated slogans and epithets designed to turn public opinion against the "stubborn," "intransigent," "reactionary," "sick old man" who "obstinately refused medical advice," was "forgotten" by his own people, was an "embarrassment" to the U.S. State Department, and an "anacronism" from the "bygone era of the cold war." Outside diplomatic pressure was continually applied to persuade the Vatican to intervene. Every spring for ten years, a spate of news stories would announce that the Cardinal would be out of Hungary "in a matter of days."

But even the most strident and persistent propaganda and high-level pressure failed to persuade Cardinal Mindszenty to leave Hungary. He steadfastly refused to accept safety and freedom for himself so long as his Hungarian people were denied *their* freedom of religion. He was always keenly aware of his responsibilities before God and man and history. He knew that his imprisonment spotlighted the hideous persecution of religion and the tragic fate of every nation under Communism. It is a characteristic of great men that they can subordinate themselves to their leadership duties. That the Cardinal always realized his unique historical role is indicated by his statement before the Communists arrested him: "Compared to the sufferings of my people, my own fate is not important."

A patriot in the highest meaning of the term, Cardinal Mindszenty identified so closely with the soul and spirit of Hungary that he could not abandon his nation still bleeding from the wounds of the Russian attack in 1956. His imprisonment in the American legation was a living reminder of the debt that Western civilization owes to Hungarians. In many speeches, Cardinal Mindszenty had repeated this theme:

"For a thousand years, our blood and our soil have defended the peace, the civilization, the culture, and the wealth of the Western world. This is why *you* could remain within the gates of life. . . . Hungarian blood flowed in streams while Michelangelo quietly conceived the dome of St. Peter's. While London enjoyed Shakespeare, Hungarians stood guard over the very gates of Rome, London and Paris. The reason England and France both have more than four times the population of Hungary is that, for centuries, Hungary has bled for the West, for the world, and for civilization."

By 1971, the atmosphere of hospitality in the American embassy in Budapest had lost its original cordiality, and the new U.S. policy calling for "an era of negotiation," rather than "an era of confrontation," made Cardinal Mindszenty no longer a welcome guest. The new mood in the U.S. State Department was that old anti-Communists such as Cardinal Mindszenty should, like old soldiers, "simply fade away."

On September 28, 1971, U.S. Ambassador Alfred Puhan terminated the American hospitality extended to the Hungarian the Communists hated the most, and led Cardinal Mindszenty out of the gray, stucco embassy on Budapest's "Freedom Square" to a car waiting at the curb. There to greet him were a Vatican aide, Monsignor Giovanni Cheli, the Hungarian-born Monsignor Joseph Zágon, and Austria's Papal Nuncio, Archbishop Opilio Rossi.

After a flight to Vienna and then to Rome, the 79-year-old Cardinal arrived at the Vatican in time for the Third Roman Synod. It was a dramatic moment when Pope Paul VI embraced him warmly and put his own pectoral cross around the Cardinal's neck.

Cardinal Mindszenty with Pope Paul VI. This picture was taken in Rome in November, 1971.

When he left Budapest, Cardinal Mindszenty made this statement: "I have decided, as a proof of my unlimited love for the Church, to leave the United States embassy. I would like to spend the rest of my life in Hungary among my people whom I love so much. But as this has become impossible, . . . I will accept what is probably the heaviest cross of my life."

For a man who had been three times arrested, who spent 8 years in Communist prisons, and 15 years as a prisoner in the American embassy, it was quite a statement to say that having to leave Hungary was "the heaviest cross of my life."

It may be that Cardinal Mindszenty will be able to serve his principles and his people better in Vienna, where he moved a few weeks later, than as a prisoner in the now-chilly climate of the U.S. embassy in Budapest. In October 1971, the Western press began circulating reports that the U.S. Government was planning to turn over the Crown of St. Stephen to the Communist rulers in Hungary. This most sacred of all Hungarian treasures was entrusted by Hungarian patriots to American troops under General George Patton in the closing weeks of World War II in order to keep it out of the hands of advancing Russian armies. It has been in a secret U.S. Government vault ever since. St. Stephen's Crown is the oldest Christian symbol of freedom and authority in Europe, dating from the year 1000 when Pope Sylvester II sent it as a gift for the crowning of Stephen I, King of Hungary.

Making use of his new freedom in Vienna, Cardinal Mindszenty on November 6 sent a confidential message to President Nixon reminding the President that he had "promised me in 1970 not to hand over . . . our holiest and greatest national relic and treasure . . . to the atheistic, illegal Hungarian regime."

After weeks of reverberations, on February 6, 1972, President Nixon, through a diplomatic representative, sent assurances to Cardinal Mindszenty that the Crown "would remain in United States safekeeping for the time being."[3]

Another important result of the Cardinal's departure from Hungary is that the way is now cleared for him to publish his own book, telling his personal story of one of the most dramatic and historic confrontations in the 20th century, and to make sure that it is accurately edited under his own supervision. He is one of the world's greatest scholars on the subject of Communism. To his lifetime study of the theory and practice of Marxism-Leninism and his extensive personal experiences, he added 15 years' research in the U.S. embassy in Budapest where one of his principal occupations was reading the Communist press and other primary sources of Communist doctrine.

The present U.S. Administration would not permit Cardinal Mindszenty to publish his memoirs so long as he was living in the U.S. embassy. Whereas the *de jure* policy of the United States, as expressed in the official Captive Nations Resolution (Public Law 86-90) and proclaimed by the U.S. President every year since 1959, is that "the enslavement of a substantial part of the world's population by Communist imperialism makes a mockery of the idea of peaceful coexistence . . . and . . . the imperialistic and aggressive policies of Russian Communism have resulted in the creation of a vast empire which poses a dire threat to the security of the United States and of all the free peoples of the world," the *de facto* policy of the present U.S. Administration is to do business with the Communist imperialists. The hallmarks of the new policy — negotiations, accommodation, detente, rapprochement, trade deals, financial credits, and treaties with the Communists — are out of tune with Cardinal Mindszenty's half-century of accurate analysis and uncompromising opposition to Communism.

Living in Vienna at the age of 80,[4] Cardinal Mindszenty still has his strong, unwrinkled face, his alert brown eyes, his vigorous speech, his sense of humor — and his steadfast principles. On Christmas Day, 1971, he said he would always be grateful to the American people for granting him hospitality in 1956, but he reminded the world: "What I have previously

Cardinal Mindszenty with Cardinal König of Austria, 1971.

condemned as evil and destructive, still is; and I will always be faithful to the principles which are necessary for the survival of Hungary and the freedom of its people."

The Communists don't often admit any errors. After Cardinal Mindszenty left Hungary, the Communist newspaper in Rome, *Paese Sera*, reluctantly admitted that the Cardinal's liberation corrected "an injustice and, above all, a political mistake."

Perhaps the Cardinal won out over the Communists, after all.

Cardinal Mindszenty at his office in Vienna, 1972.

The Diary of Sister Adelaide

Sister Adelaide, the good nun who spent so much time with Mother Mindszenty, was one of those rare individuals who kept a diary. Her diary is important not only because of her association with the Cardinal's mother, but because it provides an eyewitness account of life in Hungary during the 1950s. She gives an off-the-cuff, unedited description of how the Communists patrol Iron Curtain borders, make unjust arrests, and recruit informers in order to maintain their police-state control. Her diary also verifies the accuracy of many details and dates in my own experiences. I am grateful to Sister Adelaide for permission to quote excerpts from her diary.

JANUARY 30, 1950:

When I came home for lunch, I found a message to come to see Sister Elizabeth right away. When I saw her this afternoon, she asked me, "Are you going to return to Szombathely soon?" "I am already scheduled to go tomorrow," I answered.

"Good," Sister Elizabeth said. "Would you be willing to take on an important assignment, even if it involves some risk?" "Yes, of course, but I'd like to know what it is."

Sister Elizabeth continued: "For more than four months, we have been unable to get any information about Cardinal Mindszenty although we have searched persistently for some clues. Just recently, we found someone who had a contact with the chief administrator of prisons in the Ministry of Justice. He is personally willing to submit a petition provided it is signed by the Cardinal's mother. Will you go and get her signature?"

I answered: "I regret that I don't know the Cardinal's mother, and I am afraid that both I and the letter will end up in the hands of the secret police."

Sister Elizabeth reassured me: "Actually, it won't be such a great task. Her house can easily be located in her small village. Please at least investigate the matter. Perhaps Father Vecsey, the theology professor in Szombathely, can help. When you meet Mother Barbara, simply tell her I have sent you."

With that, she put the petition in my hands.

FEBRUARY 3, 1950:

Having just returned from Mindszent, I am glad I have a little time to record some impressions of my visit with the Primate's mother.

Monsignor Géfin, the Rector of the Seminary, and Father Vecsey, the Prefect, had told me the best way to travel and how to locate Mother Barbara's home. The bus stopped in the center of Mindszent, not far from the church. I walked straight ahead counting the houses, according to my instructions, and finally reached the one which had been carefully described for me. . . .

The door was opened by a peasant woman of medium height and delicate frame. She was dressed very neatly. She radiated so much natural poise that all my timidity vanished. I introduced myself and told her that Sister Elizabeth had sent me. As soon as I mentioned Sister Elizabeth, the trace of suspicion left her face and she became very friendly and invited me into the warm room. She listened carefully as I told her why I had come.

She read the petition, signed it, and asked me to relay her appreciation to Sister Elizabeth and to Dr. Farkas, the lawyer. . . .

The Cardinal's mother talked quite a bit that evening. She told me what great difficulties she encountered in trying to visit her son. The Government had even denied her permission to send him a Christmas package. I am sure she is keenly hurt about this, but she has such self-control that it does not show. . . .

From what she said that evening, it is obvious that she directs the entire household and is active in the care of others. I admire her abundant faith and hope in God. It occurred to me that the Cardinal's great virtues must have been planted while he lived in this quiet religious farm home, warmed by the love and faith of a wonderful woman, his mother.

I am so glad I made this trip and could meet her. I hope I see her soon again.

FEBRUARY 20, 1950:

Our Provincial Superior has been visiting in our Convent for the last two days. When we were alone today, she asked me: "Weren't you afraid that it might be dangerous to go to Mindszent?" "Yes, I was afraid at the beginning," I admitted, "but later my courage returned. After it was over, I was really glad that Sister Elizabeth trusted me with that mission."

Then she asked me, "Are you willing to make the trip again, and would you be willing to appear publicly with the Cardinal's mother?"

I didn't quite understand the way she worded her question, but I assumed it involved performing various services for the Cardinal's mother. It was obvious that my Superior wanted me to voluntarily accept this further mission. I hesitated a moment and then said: "Yes, I am ready for this service, if you will tell me what is expected and how to do it."

She told me that she had been asked by some Seminary priests to appoint a Sister to help Mother Barbara in transmitting her letters from Mindszent to Szombathely and then to Budapest. This Sister would be her constant companion on any trips she might make, and would be at her side during the night in case she needed assistance or medicine because of asthma attacks or other illness.

My Provincial Superior concluded: "If you are willing to volunteer your service, Sister, you have permission to put aside all your usual work while you are helping the Cardinal's mother. You will need self-control and serenity in carrying out your duties with her. Indeed, you will have a great opportunity to learn these virtues from her by being with her so often."

I was secretly thrilled that she gave me this assignment and felt it was a wonderful privilege.

MARCH 12, 1950:

The day before yesterday, the first message came telling me to accompany the Cardinal's mother to Budapest. I did not need to go to Mindszent this time, as she wanted me to meet her at the station in Szombathely. She arrived there in the morning after traveling for almost two hours by bus and train. She did not appear tired. Everyone says she is especially alert when she is doing anything connected with her son.

I took her to the Szombathely Seminary. The Rector, Monsignor Géfin, welcomed us, said Mass for us in the chapel, and then we had breakfast with him. Father Vecsey joined us and traveled to Budapest with us so he could talk to attorney Farkas.

It was evening when we arrived in Budapest. All three of us stayed at the Convent of the Sisters of Charity of Szatmár on Délibáb Street.

MARCH 25, 1950:

The Cardinal's mother left Budapest for Mindszent today with Father Vecsey. I regretted that I couldn't go with her. Because of Father's illness, I had to stay with Mother. I went to the railway station with Mother Barbara where she said, "If only I could learn whether my son were dead or alive!"

JUNE 20, 1950:

The night before last, some 1,000 religious were hauled away from their convents by the secret police. I escaped this fate only because I had gone with Mother Barbara to Mindszent. According to my Superior's previous instructions, I changed into secular dress and came back home to stay with my widowed mother in Budapest.

JULY 2, 1950:

Today I went to Vác to see the Sisters from my Convent who had been taken there by the secret police. I took them some food, soap and blankets. About 500 nuns from various religious communities are crowded into the Bishop's residence. Many of them sleep on straw on the floor. Bishop Pétery is helping them as much as he can. The police will not permit them to leave the building and the nuns are completely in the dark about their future. There is a rumor that they will all be sent to Siberia.

SEPTEMBER 10, 1950:

Today I obtained a certificate permitting me to work as a civilian. I have a job as a cleaning woman for a family with four pre-school children. I also help the mother teach religion to her children. She is aware of my situation and has generously given me time to teach religion in other families, too. I quickly found seven other pupils. Their parents, who are old friends, are afraid to risk losing their jobs if they send their children openly for religious instruction. I also find time to meet regularly every week with three groups of high school girls. . . .

MAY 15, 1955:

It is a long time since I have written in my diary —

almost three years. In prison we were not allowed to have any paper or pencil. My mother saved my diary from being confiscated, so now I can continue it.

To be at home! What a joy to be with Mother, to walk around freely, to open and close doors with my own hands, even to be able to turn on and off the lights!

I have not seen Mother Barbara since 1952. After I have rested a little while, I will go and visit her. . . .

In 1952, life for nearly all religious became desperate. Many of our Sisters could get jobs only as factory workers or as cleaning women and cooks in private homes. The only job one of our nuns could find was shoveling scrap iron at a steel plant in Csepel. Another nun became a street sweeper. Both had degrees in higher education. . . . Sisters in other countries invited us to continue our religious lives in freedom in the West — but that would mean taking the risk of trying to escape across the border, as the Government would not issue us any passports.

I received an invitation from a convent in another country. With two other Sisters in our religious community and a trusted guide, we started on a journey which was to take us north into Czechoslovakia, and then west across the border into Austria. We were advised to take this route because the Czechoslovakian border was not mined as heavily as the Hungarian border.

In a small canoe, we crossed the Danube River into Czechoslovakia during the night. We took a train to a small Czechoslovakian village, hid out in a peasant home for several days, and then took another train to Bratislava. There we were joined by 16 other people for the most dangerous part of the journey. Our companions were an elderly couple with their daughter and five-year-old grandson, a woman with two daughters aged 12 and 15, another couple with their 18-year-old son, a young couple with a one-year-old son who was given a sleeping pill to keep him quiet, and four other adults who desperately wanted to reach the Free World.

After sunset, we left the city on foot. We were unpleasantly surprised to find the meadows and fields covered by fresh snow. Fortunately, our guide was able to find the route he had planned. Most of the time we followed each other in single file, or two-by-two.

Our guide led us forward in the pitch blackness of a night that seemed to have no end. From time to time, we heard dogs barking in the distance and we would immediately stop. Twice we dropped flat on the ground to hide from passersby or from border guards. Just before midnight, we arrived at a triple-woven barbed-wire fence. Our guide pulled the wires apart to help each of us crawl through. After crossing some railroad tracks, we rested for a bit, as we were quite tired from hiking through the fields which were kept freshly-plowed to make it easier for the border police to catch people trying to escape.

"Within 10 minutes we will be in Austria," our guide told us, pointing in the direction of an Austrian village. We could see a light in the far distance. We pulled ourselves together to continue our trek. The guide went ahead to find the Austrian guards he was supposed to know. Obeying his instructions, we followed him single-file in a long stretched-out line leaving plenty of space between each person. We had walked only a couple of minutes when Sister Maria, who was closest to me, stopped and said, "I can't go any further. I am too tired. Leave me here. At least you can escape."

"You can't stay behind," I told her. "It is a matter of life or death."

I offered her my arm and tried to help her, but she just couldn't walk. It was like pulling a heavy rock. Meanwhile, a full moon had lighted the countryside. I looked around for our third Sister to help us. At that moment, I saw that the family in front of us, the couple with the 18-year-old son, had stopped and knelt down. We did likewise, just as our guide had instructed us before we began our flight.

Just then, a flare went up high in the sky above us. From behind us, somewhere to our right, a spray of bullets came our way. At the first fusillade, Sister Maria, who was kneeling at my right, cried out, "I'm shot." She fell to the ground, her arms stretched out toward me. I hugged the ground beside her in the snow and, instinctively, made an act of contrition.

A second flare went off, and all I could think of was that

I was not ready to die. Suddenly I had a passionate desire to live. There were two more volleys of shots, and bullets fell like hailstones all around us. Maria cried out in pain three times before I could clamp my hand over her mouth so she would not betray our position.

But it was too late. In a matter of moments we were surrounded by the Czechoslovakian border police. Their guns pointed directly at us and their police dogs were held at leash length. While I was still on the ground, the police chained my hands behind my back, then pulled me to my feet. I asked them to help Maria up. They shone their flashlights on her face, took a look, and made a negative gesture. She was dead. They left her there.

I was surrounded by three of the border guards. They led me toward another group a few yards away. I could not understand what they were saying. Then one of the guards put out his foot and tripped me so that I fell in the snow with both my hands still tied behind my back. As I looked around, I saw a sight I shall never forget.

Behind us lay the elderly couple, their daughter and grandson, and a bachelor who had helped them during our flight by carrying the five-year-old on his back. The two women were dead, lying rather close to each other. The grandfather was lying on his back, moaning in his death agony. I saw the boy for only a moment. One of the guards picked him up and carried him back to the military base. Several months later, I learned that the child had been wounded in the back by a bullet. In front of me, the bachelor who had carried the child lay on his stomach with his hands bound behind his back. His wound did not appear mortal, since he was able to lift his head and answer the soldiers. His left leg was bleeding profusely, and a soldier was trying to cut through the side of his trousers with a pocket knife.

I don't know how long I was left on the ground. Finally, three soldiers surrounded me, made me stand up, and made me walk toward the nearest guard house. After a few steps, we could hear a motor. "What is it?" I asked. From behind, a guard answered casually in Hungarian, "The car coming to pick up the dead and injured."

A few minutes later, we approached the guard house. Suddenly, the soldier behind me pulled the shawl off my head and blindfolded me with it. I was led on in the blackness.

Stories of other people's experiences at the border flashed through my mind. I was afraid they would execute me, just stand me up against the wall and then shoot. But that didn't happen. They rechained my hands in front of me instead of behind. Still blindfolded, I was led up some stairs, We entered a room and they seated me at the end of a bench. First there was dead silence, and of course, I couldn't see anything. Suddenly, a woman started to moan. I was terrified, but soon figured out from the conversation that she was suffering severe pain in her feet, which were frozen from her long walk. I gathered that others from our group had also been caught trying to cross the border and had been brought into this building.

I sat quietly, trying to guess what would happen next. Soon I was led into another room. I had to give my personal data while still blindfolded. Then I was returned to my bench. The guards removed the blindfold for the second interrogation and questioned me closely on how I got from Budapest to the border. In a side room, I was thoroughly searched. Interrogations were repeated several times during the day.

It was late afternoon before a guard permitted me to take off my blindfold for good. Then I saw that five companions of our flight were near me: the woman with her son, and the two young girls with their mother. We were not permitted to talk. One guard seemed to be sorry for us. He took the chains off our wrists and loaned us his comb. They gave us each a small amount of soup, but none of us had any appetite. In the meantime, they typed up the answers we had given to the interrogations. After we had signed them, we were allowed to lie down on the benches to sleep.

The next morning very early, we were taken in locked prison vans to the Bratislava city jail. A month later, our trial took place. The sentence was 60 days in prison for trying to cross the Czechoslovakian-Austrian border without passports. We were also told that, after our jail term ended, we would be handed over to the Hungarian Communists for an additional prison term for leaving Hungary without permission.

But nothing changed after 60 days were up. We were kept in prison for more than a year in complete uncertainty, except that after six months the two young girls were released under house arrest to local relatives until they, too, were turned over to the Hungarian border police.

In prison, I worked at various jobs: cleaning feathers, peeling onions, cleaning prison offices and corridors, washing laundry, and working in the kitchen. At the beginning of our term, each of us received a prisoner's number and was photographed in our prison uniform, holding our number in front of us. Each of us ceased to be a person and was known only by a number. Part of our punishment was to make us feel cast out from society.

During this year in prison, only Divine Providence helped me retain my sanity and humanity. I had been in prison for about four months when some 30 Catholic priests were transferred from another jail to ours. I was washing the corridor when they arrived and I stepped aside to let them go through. When the guards were out of earshot, I whispered to the priests, "Jesus Christ be praised!" One priest gave a cautious answer without moving his lips.

A few days later, I saw this same priest go alone through the corridor to the office. We were able to exchange a few words. He told me some priests managed to offer Mass secretly, and he promised to bring me the Blessed Sacrament the following day.

The next day I was washing the windows of the corridor when he passed by. He quickly gave me the Blessed Sacrament which had been neatly folded in a piece of white paper. I placed it in a pocket of my prison slacks and continued working. Nobody noticed anything.

During the rest of the day, I continued my window cleaning, devoting my thoughts to meditation and adoration of Jesus in preparation for receiving Holy Communion the following morning. It was a great consolation to know that Christ was my Companion not only in the peaceful Convent, but even in this wretched prison.

In the morning, before the guards came to inspect our cells, my cellmate and I knelt down and said the Confiteor. Then I broke the Blessed Sacrament, gave her half and myself the remainder. The guards never noticed.

Once again a few days later, I received Holy Communion the same way. Then a few of the priests were freed, and all the others were taken to various other prisons.

From time to time, three other young women prisoners (who were also captured at the border trying to escape) and I were taken to clean various other buildings occupied by police personnel. This was a welcome change for us, since we were driven in ordinary cars instead of closed, locked-up prison vans. We rode through the city streets and got a brief look at what life was like on the outside. We were driven through town on Holy Thursday and happened to pass in front of a church. Its door was open and for a fleeting moment we could see the Blessed Sacrament surrounded by candles, white flowers, and beautiful decorations.

Since we worked in teams and had a frequent change of cellmates, I came to know some of the prisoners very well, especially those who were Hungarian. During my year in prison, I met more than 80 fellow Hungarians who had tried to escape through Czechoslovakia into Austria. They had requested passports, but the Rákosi Government had refused to issue them. Before they could reach freedom, they were captured by the Communist police in Czechoslovakia. Their fate was similar to mine, that is, they were kept in a Czechoslovakian prison for an indefinite period and then handed back to the Hungarian Communists for an additional sentence. We were of all ages and walks of life, and all jammed together in a miserable prison. The youngest was a 15-year-old student.

The oldest was a 72-year old widow who had escaped deportation in 1951 by swimming across the wide Danube into Czechoslovakia. [That was the year when the Hungarian Government carried out mass deportations from the larger cities in order to eliminate the educated non-Communist middle class.] She had managed to take with her a few jewels and a small amount of money. She desperately wanted to reach her children in West Germany. For several months, she tried to find a guide who would lead her across the border into Austria. She spent many nights sleeping under the bushes in public parks, in the waiting rooms at railroad stations, or in places the poor were permitted to use in bitter cold weather. Finally, she found a man who agreed to help her for a certain price. After pocketing his fee, he led her straight into the hands of the Czechoslovakian border police!

Another of my prison companions, a young girl of 18, used to work in a mine and was a Stakhanovite [a worker rewarded for exceeding production quotas]. She had tried to escape to join relatives in faraway Australia, but she too had been captured. Another woman with her 14-year-old daughter had tried to join her husband in Austria, from whom they had been separated for years. They, too, had their hopes dashed by prison.

I had all different kinds of cellmates. Once I shared a cell with six young prostitutes. I felt so sorry for them after hearing them talk about their miserable lives. At another time, I shared a large cell with 14 other inmates, all from the local vicinity. There was the young seamstress who had murdered her illegitimate child, the high school language teacher who had been reported to the police by her 14-year-old pupils for behavior "contrary to the State," the rural midwife who had performed illegal abortions, the young woman who had hidden her own money when her family store was taken over by the State, the girl who had tried to escape to the West by plane with her fiancé who was a pilot, and the young woman who had tried to cross the border with her dentist husband. After capture, she was beaten so cruelly by the police that she lost her baby.

It is so painful to remember the faces of my cellmates — and all those lives which turned out so differently from the way they were planned. . . .

My most depressing recollection is the period when I was confined to a cell whose only window overlooked the prison yard where executions of political prisoners were carried out each Tuesday and Friday morning at 5:00 A.M. As we were on a higher floor, we could not see the scaffold or the hangman's noose, but the noises and voices would usually awaken us. I would always pray for the doomed. Only once was someone released from Death Row. He was a teenager who had committed a murder a year before but, according to the law, could be executed only when he reached his 18th birthday.

These prison experiences helped me to realize that everything on earth has value only in the light of eternity. Whatever cannot be made to serve our passage to eternal life, is not worthy of our attachment. We must always be ready to give an account of our actions. . . .

We tried to make Christmas a happy occasion. At that time, ten of us worked in the prison laundry. One was a Franciscan Sister who had been a nurse in a large hospital. She had been condemned to two and a half years' imprisonment because she did not comply with the law for reporting all persons to the police. Her Franciscan friends sent her a food parcel in which they had hidden a branch of a fir tree and a postcard showing the stable in Bethlehem. We were allowed to have our Christmas supper right in the laundry room. The guards permitted us to put together two long laundry tables. We covered them with clean sheets, placed the Bethlehem picture and the pine branch as a centerpiece, and knelt in prayer before this Nativity scene. Then we wished each other a Merry Christmas and ate our fried fish.

Later, as our guards led us across the snow-covered yard back to our cells in the other building, we could hear from the other side of the building the male prisoners singing softly but distinctly, "Silent Night, Holy Night." It was rare for any voice ever to penetrate our prison walls. Under that clear sky studded with radiant stars, on that snowy winter night in the prison yard, I recalled the Introit for the Sunday within the Octave of Christmas: "For while all things were in quiet silence, and the night was in the midst of her course, Thy almighty Word leapt down from Heaven from Thy royal throne." . . .

Thirteen months had passed since our arrest. Suddenly, one winter morning, we were not taken to the laundry. Our baggage and civilian clothes were returned. We were told to change and get ready because, within an hour, we were to be turned over to Hungarian officials. Before noon we reached a Hungarian police station on the border.

Our Hungarian guards were kind young lads. While we had to wait for hours, they told us not to be sad because we would not be locked up too much longer. In the past year, they said, political conditions had changed for the better.

Before midnight, a huge van for transporting prisoners arrived. The next morning, the 16 of us were sent to the secret police prison on Main Street in Budapest. Here our group was split up and our interrogation started all over again. Photographs and fingerprints were taken. Bright lights shone day and night in our cells. We were awakened frequently during the night. All our personal items such as hairpins, shoelaces and stockings were confiscated. All the prisoners on one floor shared a common towel and comb. This was the same kind of treatment we had already encountered from the secret police in Czechoslovakia.

Ten days later we were transferred to the prison on Markó Street. Then a trial took place which was closed to the public. I was sentenced to two and a half years in prison for crossing the border without a passport. The 13 months I had already served in Bratislava was accepted as part of my prison term.

The thing I remember best about the Markó Street prison was hunger. Nobody had a job. We received such poor food that one of my cellmates put mentholated toothpaste on her bread. The temperature was very cold. We were on the fourth floor and the central heating didn't reach that far up.

It was quite an experience to hear about the lives of two of my cellmates. One was a Hungarian, the other a young Greek woman. Both had been members of the Communist Party since they were 15 years old, and both had been cast into prison by their Party bosses. The Hungarian woman had even been deprived of her Party membership, but continued to speak enthusiastically about Communism.

After two months, I was transferred to another prison out in the rural countryside. There were about 800 women prisoners there, half for political reasons, half for ordinary crimes. Our treatment was similar to the other prisons I had been in. As the warden remarked: "You convicts are third-class beings."

Here, however, we could apply for work, and I took advantage of that opportunity. We worked hard at our jobs and even overproduced in order to gain various benefits. The prison warden had a calculated method of exploiting prison labor. Those exceeding production quotas received special privileges such as permission to receive a letter, a gift parcel, or even a visitor. A five per cent surplus over the daily work quota was rewarded by a one-day reduction of the prisoner's jail sentence. With God's help, I "overworked" so that I was released 25 days earlier than my prison sentence called for.

It was daybreak when I was released from the prison in Kalocsa. I walked through the empty streets to the Cathedral. Its doors were not yet open. I knelt on the step in front of the locked front gate and thanked God for helping me to survive. Then I hurried to catch the bus for Budapest to get home to Mother as soon as possible.

NOVEMBER 1, 1956:

Wonderful, exciting days!

Freedom! This word has become a reality for us! Everything is in turmoil, but we are filled with hope, though there will still have to be many sacrifices to realize our great dreams. . . .

I have just returned from the funeral of one of our Sisters. She lived in a house opposite Budapest's radio station. On her return from work the evening of October 23, a stray bullet fired from the radio station building struck her while in her own apartment. Her roommate found her unconscious on the floor. She died three days later.

At my home, I found a message from the Cardinal. I am to carry a letter to his dear mother in Mindszent. I am more than willing; I am overjoyed to do this.

MARCH 31, 1957:

Oh, the horrible days I have had to go through. . . .

Three weeks ago, sometime after 10:00 P.M., just after we had gone to bed and put out the light, the doorbell rang. I hurriedly put on a coat and went to the door. The janitor of our apartment building was standing there with four strangers. They said they had a warrant to search our apartment and take me into custody. They showed me the written warrant. Then they started to ransack all my belongings, throwing everything about pell-mell. They didn't say a word about what they were searching for. I had no idea what they wanted.

They stopped their search after about an hour and after having taken possession of a single issue of the *Sacred Heart* magazine published about the end of October 1956. Mother and I watched them in silence. What could they possibly hope to find? At the end of their search, they told me to get dressed and be ready to be taken away by them. I asked in vain where they were taking me. They would not answer.

They led me to their car. It was about midnight when we arrived at a building I did not recognize. There was a long corridor on the main floor. Facing one wall stood a row of men, and facing the opposite wall was a row of women. I was ordered to join the group of women and face the wall. We all had to stand in dead silence for what seemed an eternity. The only sounds were the steps of the guards and the abrupt commands given to the prisoners brought in after I was.

Suddenly, a prison guard ordered four of us women to follow him. He put us in a very small cell which contained two sleeping cots and a toilet bowl. We hardly had room to turn around. After the door was locked behind us, my companions burst into indignant and frightened expletives.

All talking at once, they told how their homes had been ransacked as they were arrested. Based on my previous experiences, I could guess what kind of treatment was in store for us. I tried to persuade them to sleep so we would be rested for the next day's interrogations. Under such miserable and crowded conditions, however, we only slept a little toward dawn.

My companions were taken first for interrogation. Each time they returned from a session, they were more upset and frightened. They did not dare to talk openly. On the second day, one of them could not contain herself any longer, saying: "They demand that I spy for them. I have a husband and two small daughters. I just don't know what to do!" The other two women were given the same kind of mental torture to persuade them to become spies.

My own interrogation took place on the third day. I was prepared for the worst and was not disappointed. A female interrogator received me in a dirty, stinking prison cell. From her opening remarks, I was given no clue as to what crime I might have committed to cause this arrest. Finally, she mentioned Mother Barbara's name. My interrogator asked me how I had happened to meet her, what connection I had with her, what she said to me after her visits with the Cardinal, and to whom I had spoken about these things, etc., etc. Then, she handed me pen and paper and ordered me to write down all my answers. With this, she ended my day's interrogation and left me alone.

The next day I was left alone, but the following day I was taken by a guard into that filthy cell again. A flood of angry words greeted me. Was I aware that I was a dangerous criminal? That I had kept contact with persons who were enemies of the people? That, if the secret police were not so benevolent toward me, they could easily prove that I had committed the crime of treason? Moreover, she threatened that the most severe punishment was in store for me.

The following day, my guard led me into a small office which was clean and bright. There were fresh flowers in a vase, a doily on the table, and a few pictures (rather cheap art) on the wall. My interrogator told me to sit down. She started with a statement that, although I was a great criminal, she wanted to help me. She was quite willing to set me free if I were willing to do what she wanted. She was eager to help free me in exchange for certain services.

My interrogator said these services would not be difficult. I was simply to carefully observe everyone at my place of work and at other places where I usually went. We would meet together in a small cafeteria from time to time, and I would report to her about everything I observed. She would give me directives and points of information to facilitate my reporting. In return for this help, she said she could not promise me a better job or a raise because that might provoke the suspicions of others, and I might lose their confidence. However, she said she would help me get some extra money and even a passport so I might take a vacation in another country. She held out the lure of other benefits, too, if I proved I was working to her satisfaction.

She said she wanted to impress on me how my entire fate depended upon her offer and my decision. She said that my reply was crucially important. She must have seen my dismay, because she closed the interview by saying she did not want an immediate decision. She told me to think it over until our next meeting. She gave me two bars of chocolate to emphasize her good will. I shared them with my remaining cellmate. The other two had been released in the meantime — we guessed for what price. . . .

Hours of agony followed. What would be Mother's fate if I refused the offer? If I accepted the offer, I would offend God, abandon my own self-respect, and betray all my friends. My one remaining roommate was released the next day, full of tears and very nervous. She also lived with a widowed mother who was gravely ill at the time of the arrest. My cellmate felt she had to pay any price in order to return home to her mother.

In my agony, I received an unexpected answer to my dilemma. A guard suddenly opened every cell on my floor, one after the other. About 30 of us were led to the large shower room on the main floor. While dressing, I looked about cautiously to see if there might be anyone I knew. Just beside me I saw one of the Sisters from my own Convent. Talking was strictly prohibited. I bent down and, without moving my lips, whispered, "How did you get here?"

Her answer was a familiar one: "There was a search at my home a week ago and I was brought here." She then told me the names of two of our fellow Sisters who had also been arrested and brought to this prison.

"Did they ask you to become their spy?" I asked. "Yes," she replied. "And what did you answer?" "No! Of course not! I wouldn't do it," she said firmly.

We had to stop our whispering because the guards were ordering us to return to our cells. However, this short conversation restored my courage. At my next interrogation, I remained resolute despite every promise and threat. My interrogator was very disappointed in me. She called in another associate. They both shouted that I was stupid and a coward and that I would be kept in prison. They said I would not be permitted even to attend my mother's funeral. They said this was my last chance. But I adamantly resisted all their offers.

After this interrogation, I was put in solitary confinement in a small cell for a week. During that time, I was allowed to walk about for only ten minutes on only one day. Toward the end of the week, I was led to an office in the prison. Two nuns from other communities whom I had known in the past were also present. All three of us were given a bundle containing prison clothes with orders to put them on the next morning, as we were to be taken to another prison.

That same afternoon, however, the guard reappeared and took me to my interrogator. She reiterated that I was a coward and stupid, and that the Communist system was strong, and then, to my utter surprise, said that they weren't afraid to let me go free despite my crimes! I had to sign a paper acknowledging that I would face two to five years of imprisonment if I ever spoke to anyone about the content of my interrogation. I was also told that I would be permitted to leave my home only for work and that I would be closely supervised by the police at all times. The following afternoon, I was finally released.

JUNE 12, 1957:

The Ministry of the Interior has notified me that I have been placed under police surveillance. I was forced to sign a notice which contained the lines: ". . . Reason for being placed under police surveillance: She endangers the security of the State and the people."

JUNE 20, 1959:

After two years, I finally received today a notice of the termination of police surveillance. Those who have never experienced day-and-night police surveillance cannot possibly understand what a nerve-racking harassment and terrible annoyance this is.

Many nights, my poor mother had to suffer with me while we endured all those unexpected police visits. In addition to those nighttime disturbances, I was obliged to report personally every Sunday morning at a certain hour to the district police station. If I wanted to go beyond the city limits of Budapest, I had to get a special written permit from the police.

I have not seen the Cardinal's mother for seven years. Because of the way the secret police watch me, I have not dared even to write her. I wish I could visit with her, but I know I must patiently wait. I don't want a visit from me to cause her any trouble.

FEBRUARY 10, 1960:

I have just received the news that Mother Barbara has died at her home in Mindszent. I have been looking at her picture taken ten years ago. I am awed by her face. . . . What a strong will, never succumbing to any obstacle or difficulty. And what goodness and devoted love burned within the heart of this frail, saintly mother who suffered so much. . . .

She has reached her goal. I trust she is praying in the presence of God that her son may be permitted to fulfill his great mission to his people.

Tribute by Bishop McNulty

"Whatever I have become is due to the merits and prayers of my mother." With these words, Joseph Cardinal Mindszenty, Primate of Hungary, intrepid martyr of the Faith, paid tribute to his mother. It is love without measure — a beautiful love, a mutual love.

His remarkable mother nourished his body at the dining table on the farm in Mindszent. She was an excellent cook and the food was abundant. Gentle courtesies made all feel at home and guests were eager to come back again. Young Joseph enjoyed his mother's cooking, the friendly atmosphere, and the stimulating conversation. Most of all, he was inspired by his mother's insight into Divine Truth.

Cardinal Mindszenty's mother loved her faith and served Our Lord in the Church with intense loyalty. The day of Father Joseph's ordination to the sacred priesthood was a day of happiness borrowed from Heaven for both mother and son. But his priestly assignment was to persecution. Soon after ordination, a reign of horror came upon his native Hungary, which is clearly identified as atheistic Communism.

Father Joseph Mindszenty had complete contempt for Communist threats. He rejected Communist doctrine. He refused even the least compromise with this evil. His mother's love and wise counsel sustained him in his steadfast resistance. His pastorate of 25 years at Zalaegerszeg was harassed by the enemies of the Church. Yet he succeeded in providing his parishioners a pastoral service of top quality.

Monsignor Mindszenty anticipated the pastoral emphasis of Vatican II. He was a good shepherd who knew his flock — and his flock knew him. His huge success as a pastor of souls brought the enmity of the atheists, but also earned for him the office of Bishop. His mother was so proud of the new Bishop as he proclaimed: "I stand firmly for God, Church and

Country in my historic responsibility to the nation which has repeatedly stood alone against the enemies of Western civilization."

His mother hungered for hope that things would get better, but she knew in her heart that, the higher the ecclesiastical honor, the heavier the cross. When her son was elevated to the highest rank, Archbishop of Esztergom and Cardinal Primate of Hungary, the honor brought her concern rather than contentment. When friends would plead with the Cardinal to go to Rome for safety's sake, he replied: "A pastor of souls must stay with his flock and cannot flee like a hired servant."

The Hungarian bishops loyally supported their Primate, but a small group of priests formed a national priests' alliance and became the trumpeters of Government policy. Impatient with the progress of the Church, these priests promoted social development rather than the Word of God. Saddened by this betrayal, the Cardinal's mother prayed: "God grant that the world will recognize the danger of Communism."

As he approached the critical days of his struggle, he told his mother: "I know very well that my arrest and perhaps execution by the Communists would break your heart. For a long time I have prayed to the Sorrowful Mother to give you the grace to accept God's will about my sufferings and death." His heroic mother watched the arrest the day after Christmas in 1948 and 59 days of horror for the Cardinal and anguish for his mother passed before they met again.

Cardinal Mindszenty is the symbol of the defense of the human freedoms which are essential for the dignity of man. The price he had to pay is incredible: physical and psychological torture, "treatment" with drugs designed to damage his mind and will, and a mock trial. All these sufferings underscore the depravity of Communism — and his heroic loyalty to God, to the Church and to his fellow men. Cardinal Mindszenty's career is for the Universal Church. It is his struggle for the Christian way of life.

After 23 years of forced silence, His Eminence prepared a Pastoral Letter for Christmas 1971. We were curious to know what he felt important after all his experiences. This is what he emphasized: "To have charity in action toward the needy is indispensable. No one may permit himself to be indifferent to the needs of others."

Cardinal Mindszenty speaks of the charity which strengthens the Church of Christ. He counsels no compromise with evil, not even the least compromise. He urges a stalwart faith nourished by charity: "Love one another as I have loved you."

Do not be afraid of the Cross. God is near.

James A. McNulty
Bishop of Buffalo, New York

REFERENCES

1. The First Imprisonment

1. Joseph Mindszenty, *Az Édesanya* (Zalaegerszeg, Vol. I, 1941; Vol. II, 1942), Vol. I, p. 374. This Hungarian work is hereafter cited under its English title, *The Mother*.

3. Father Mindszenty the Author

1. Joseph Vecsey, *Mindszenty Okmánytár* (Munich, 1957), Vol. I, p. 18. This 3-volume Hungarian work, whose English title is *Documentation Concerning Cardinal Mindszenty*, is hereafter cited as *Documentation*.
2. *Ibid.*, Vol. I, p. 85.
3. *Ibid.*, Vol. I, pp. 85-87.
4. *The Mother, op. cit.*, Vol. I, p. 266.
5. *Ibid.*, Vol. I, p. 239.
6. *Ibid.*, Vol. I, pp. 326-327.
7. *Ibid.*, Vol. I, p. 227.
8. *Ibid.*, Vol. I, pp. 327-328.

4. Imprisonment by the Nazis

1. The complete statement of Ladislaus Endre, Department Head, and other pertinent documents, appear in *Documentation, op. cit.*, Vol. III, p. 17.
2. An excellent account of Cardinal Mindszenty's lifetime of respect for and defense of the rights of the Jews is told by a Hungarian member of the Jewish congregation, Béla Fabian, in his book, *Cardinal Mindszenty: The Story of a Modern Martyr* (New York, Charles Scribner's Sons, 1949).
3. The complete text of the Bishop's memorandum is given in *Documentation*, Vol. I, pp. 20-21.
4. *Ibid.*, Vol. I, pp. 206-207.
5. *Ibid.*, Vol. I, p. 87.

5. Manning the Fortresses

1. Donald Sulyok in his book *Hungarian Tragedy* was incomplete in reporting the details of his release from the Kanizsa concentration camp. Overestimating his own importance, Sulyok failed to mention that Bishop Mindszenty had interceded on his behalf to make possible his daughter's marriage. The groom was an officer, and the military authorities would not permit him to marry the daughter of a political prisoner. While visiting the town of Pápa, Bishop

Mindszenty was asked to intervene by Mrs. Sulyok and the women members of the local Marian association. Sulyok was interceded for, not as a politician, but as a parent.

2. *The Mother, op. cit.,* Vol. II, p. 367.
3. In the spring of 1946, Father Töhötöm Nagy allowed the KALOT to be maneuvered into joining MIOT, the leading Communist youth organization. The local affiliates of the KALOT, however, heroically refused to cooperate with the Communists. When the Russians observed this, they dissolved the entire KALOT organization. Their excuse was the murder of a Russian soldier on Theresa Boulevard in Budapest. He had been shot and killed by another Russian soldier in a drunken brawl. The murdered soldier was buried with full military honors. At the funeral, the commander-in-chief of the Soviet occupation forces in Hungary falsely charged that an ungrateful KALOT youth had murdered a heroic soldier of the "Army of Liberation." In retaliation the Russians henceforth demanded that the Cabinet of Ferenc Nagy dissolve all non-Communist youth organizations, which the Cabinet did.

   Father Töhötöm Nagy desperately attempted, with the help of his Russian friends, to have the KALOT dropped from the list of organizations to be dissolved. Many weeks after his request, he received an answer stipulating that the KALOT would be excepted if its name were changed, new leaders elected from a list of Communist-approved candidates, its bylaws rewritten in accordance with Communist demands, and a promise given to "cooperate fully" with the Communist MIOT. Father Nagy agreed to all these demands, but the local groups abandoned it and the KALOT disintegrated.

   Meanwhile, Father Nagy began openly to criticize the Church and the Vatican, and continued to cooperate with the Communist secret police. The Jesuits transferred him to South America, where he finally left the Order, became a Mason, and was married.

4. *Documentation, op. cit.,* Vol. I, p. 42.
5. *Ibid.,* Vol. I, pp. 48-49.
6. *The Mother, op. cit.,* Vol. II, p. 17.
7. *Documentation,* Vol. I, p. 49.
8. *Ibid.,* Vol. I, p. 127.
9. *Ibid.,* Vol. I, p. 66.
10. *Ibid.,* Vol. I, pp. 120-121.
11. *Ibid.,* Vol. I, p. 142.
12. *Ibid.,* Vol. I, pp. 245-246.
13. *Ibid.,* Vol. I, p. 266.
14. *Ibid.,* Vol. III, p. 78.
15. *Ibid.,* Vol. II, pp. 277-280.
16. The 1947 Marian festivities and pilgrimages are described in *Documentation,* Vol. III, pp. 61-112.

17. The 1948 Marian celebrations are described in *Documentation,* Vol. III, pp. 203-246.

18. The character of General Voroshilov is illustrated by a conversation he had in the Kremlin with American Ambassador William C. Bullitt, which was quoted in an article by the founder of the Cardinal Mindszenty Foundation, Father C. Stephen Dunker, C.M., in *Our Sunday Visitor,* July 22, 1962. This article was awarded a George Washington Honor Medal by the Freedoms Foundation at Valley Forge, Pennsylvania. Here is the conversation:

    Voroshilov: "I think the most extraordinary thing we did was to capture Kiev without fighting."

    Bullitt: "How did that happen?"

    Voroshilov: "Well, there were 11,000 Czarist officers with their wives and children in Kiev and they had more troops than we had, and we never could have captured the city by fighting. So we used propaganda and we told them that they would be released and allowed to go to their homes with their families and would be treated as well as possible by our army. They believed and surrendered."

    Bullitt: "What did you do then?"

    Voroshilov: "Oh, we shot the men and boys, and we put all the women and girls in brothels for our army."

    Bullitt: "Do you think that was a very decent thing to do?"

    Voroshilov: "My army needed women and I was concerned with my army's health and not with the health of those women. And it didn't make any difference anyhow, because the women were all dead in three months."

19. The first attacks against Catholic education are described in *Documentation,* Vol. I, pp. 150-160; and Vol. II, pp. 17-77. The violent attacks against religious teaching in schools are described in *Documentation,* Vol. II, pp. 147-187.

20. The struggle to preserve Catholic schools is described in *Documentation,* Vol. III, pp. 115-193.

6. The Gathering Storm

1. *Documentation, op. cit.,* Vol. III, pp. 133-134.
2. *Ibid.,* Vol. III, pp. 227-229.

8. The Third Arrest

1. *Documentation, op. cit.,* Vol. III, pp. 261-262.
2. *Ibid.,* Vol. III, p. 264.
3. *Ibid.,* Vol. III, p. 265.
4. *Ibid.,* Vol. III, p. 266.
5. *Ibid.,* Vol. III, pp. 275-277.

6. The correspondence about the Crown of St. Stephen had started in the entourage of the exiled Regent, Admiral Horthy. These Hungarian refugees were eager to secure permanent safety for this most sacred of all Hungarian relics. Admiral Horthy and the other exiles asked the Pope and Cardinal Mindszenty to request that this precious national relic be transferred to the Vatican from the U.S. Army (to which Hungarian soldiers had entrusted it in the final months of World War II). This was the origin of the Cardinal's correspondence in September 1947 which the Communists used to fabricate their charges of "monarchism" and "conspiracy against the Republic."
7. *Documentation*, Vol. III, pp. 282-285.

9. The Mock Trial

1. Sister Elizabeth's article, entitled "Mother, You Found Me Even Here!" was published in the newspaper, *Életünk*, January 1, 1969.
2. *Documents on the Mindszenty Case* (Budapest, January 1949).
3. *Documentation, op. cit.*, Vol. III, p. 287.
4. The entire dossier of the Cardinal's trial was published by the Hungarian Communist Government in the so-called *Black Book*. The English title of this volume is *Joseph Mindszenty Before The People's Court* (Budapest, Hungarian State Publishing House, 1949). A good account of the Cardinal's interrogation, treatment with drugs, and trial is given in *The Cardinal's Story* by Stephen K. Swift (New York, Macmillan Company, 1950).
5. P. Beat Ambord, S.J., *Der Vatikan und die Kirche hinter dem Eisernem Vorhang* (Rome, 1949), p. 78.
6. *Free Nation* (newspaper), February 2, 1949.

10. The Cardinal Disappears

1. *Documentation, op. cit.*, Vol. III, p. 285.
2. *L'Osservatore Romano*, January 4, 1949.
3. P. Beat Ambord, *op. cit.*, pp. 72-73.
4. *Documentation*, Vol. III, pp. 286-287.
5. The letters from which these excerpts are taken were written by the Cardinal's mother between 1949 and 1956 to a friend in New York City. Their recipient made the originals available to me. Other parts of these letters have been quoted in the book by George N. Shuster, *In Silence I Speak* (New York, Farrar, Straus & Cudahy, 1956), pp. 79-86.

12. Visitation at Vác

1. Joseph Mindszenty was ordained in Szombathely on June 12, 1915.

13. The Agreement

1. *Documentation, op. cit.,* Vol. III, p. 300.
2. The text of this letter, which was also a forgery, is printed in *Documentation,* Vol. III, pp. 292-293.
3. *Institute de Recherches de l'Europe Central* (IREC), Louvain, Dossier B, 3/a.
4. *IREC,* Dossier B, 3/c.
5. *IREC,* Dossier B, 4/b.
6. *IREC,* Dossier B, 4/c and B, 4/e.
7. *IREC,* Dossier B, 4/f and B, 4/g.

14. More Years in Prison

1. *Hungarian Courier,* July 5, 1951.
2. *Ibid.,* September 21, 1951.
3. *Ibid.,* October 20, 1951.

16. A Refugee in His Own Country

1. The reporter for Reuters News Agency was inadvertently misled by Communist news sources into announcing that the Cardinal's radio message had demanded the return of expropriated Church lands, based on a mistranslation of the expression "Church institution" as "Church property." In Hungarian, the word "institution" never means landed property.
2. The whole text of the letter is published in *Documentation, op. cit.,* Vol. III, pp. 315-316.
3. New York *Times,* February 9, 1972.
4. Cardinal Mindszenty was born March 29, 1892.

Cardinal Mindszenty with Father Joseph Vecsey. This picture was taken at St. Stephen's Church in Vienna, November 21, 1971. It was Cardinal Mindszenty's first public Mass after 15 years in the American Embassy in Budapest.

JOSEPH VECSEY

Joseph Vecsey is the editor of *Mindszenty Okmánytár* *(Documentation Concerning Cardinal Mindszenty)*, Munich, 1957, a three-volume work published in both Hungarian and German. He is also the co-author of *Kardinal Mindszenty: Das Gewissen der Welt* (*Cardinal Mindszenty: The Conscience of the World*), Würzburg, 1972.

Dr. Vecsey received his Doctor of Divinity degree from Pázmány University in Budapest and was ordained a Catholic priest in 1938. He was a high school religion teacher in Zalaegerszeg from 1939 to 1942, and Prefect of the Preparatory Seminary in Szombathely from 1942 to 1945. From 1946 to 1952, he was Prefect and Professor at the Theological Seminary in Szombathely.

Father Vecsey escaped from Hungary in 1952. He studied Church Law at the Angelicum University in Rome, and in 1954 and 1955 was the chief religion writer for Radio Free Europe in Munich. He now lives in Switzerland where he edits a newspaper for Hungarians in Europe.

Beginning at the age of ten, Dr. Vecsey has had a lifetime of friendship and association with Cardinal Mindszenty. This book is based on eyewitness experiences and on careful notes Dr. Vecsey has made and collected ever since 1934.

PHYLLIS SCHLAFLY

Phyllis Schlafly is the author of *A Choice Not An Echo* and *Safe — Not Sorry,* and the co-author with Admiral Chester Ward of three books on nuclear strategy, *The Grave-diggers, Strike From Space,* and *The Betrayers.*

Mrs. Schlafly writes a monthly newsletter called *The Phyllis Schlafly Report.* Her series of interviews with European and American experts on the Communist military threat to the Free World has been aired on 70 television and 50 radio stations. She has repeatedly testified on national security and Communist propaganda before the Senate Armed Forces and Foreign Relations Committees. She is a frequent speaker on college campuses and to national audiences.

Mrs. Schlafly worked her way through college, receiving her A.B. with Honors in three years from Washington University, election to Phi Beta Kappa, and a Master's Degree from Harvard University. She lives with her husband and their six children on a bluff overlooking the Mississippi River in Alton, Illinois. She is the recipient of many awards including the *St. Louis Globe-Democrat* award for Woman of Achievement in Public Affairs, and three George Washington Honor Medals from Freedoms Foundation at Valley Forge.

CARDINAL MINDSZENTY FOUNDATION

The Cardinal Mindszenty Foundation is an international, non-profit, educational organization whose purpose is to provide the public with reliable information on the problems posed by Communism. It was named in honor of Joseph Cardinal Mindszenty, who is a worldwide symbol of uncompromising resistance to Communism.

The Foundation's educational program includes study courses, lectures, films, printed materials, conferences, and radio programs on the nature of Communism, its propaganda and objectives. Over the years, CMF has had at least 5,000 study groups. Its award-winning radio program, "Dangers of Apathy," has been heard on hundreds of stations.

The Cardinal Mindszenty Foundation was founded in 1958 by Father C. Stephen Dunker, C.M. It is governed by the Cardinal Mindszenty Council whose membership is limited to Cardinals, bishops and priests who have lived under Communism in some part of the world. The following Council members have had first-hand experience with the Communists in Russia, China, Hungary, Lithuania, Ghana, Vietnam, Laos, Korea, Tibet or Cuba:

His Eminence, Paul Cardinal Yu Pin *(China)*
Archbishop of Nanking

His Eminence, Thomas Cardinal Tien, S.V.D.† *(China)*
Archbishop of Peking

Most Rev. Vincent Brizgys *(Lithuania)*
Auxiliary Bishop of Kaunas

Most Rev. John A. Choi *(Korea)*
Bishop of Pusan

Most Rev. Rembert C. Kowalski, O.F.M.† *(China)*
Bishop of Wuchang

Most Rev. Thomas Niu *(China)*
Bishop of Yanku

Most Rev. Cuthbert M. O'Gara, C.P.† *(China)*
Bishop of Yuanling

Most Rev. John A. O'Shea, C.M.† *(China)*
Bishop of Kanchow

Rt. Rev. Eugene E. Fahy, S.J. *(China)*

Rt. Rev. Joseph Zágon *(Hungary)*

Very Rev. Warren F. Dicharry, C.M. *(China)*

Very Rev. Bernard M. Druetto, O.F.M. *(China)*

Very Rev. John J. Kelly, O.S.A. *(Cuba)*

Very Rev. Ladislas Keresztesy Parker, O. Praem. *(Hungary)*

Very Rev. Harold W. Rigney, S.V.D. *(China)*

Rev. Leopold Braun, A.A.† *(Russia)*

Rev. Francis X. Clougherty, O.S.B. *(China)*

Rev. Paul Coquoz *(Tibet)*

Rev. Robert Crawford, C.M. *(China and Vietnam)*

Rev. Raymond J. deJaegher *(China and Vietnam)*

Rev. Juan M. Dorta-Duque, S.J. *(Cuba)*

Rev. Paul Duchesne, M.M. *(China)*

Rev. C. S. Dunker, C.M. *(China)*

Rev. Joseph J. Hill, C.M. *(China)*

Rev. John A. Houle, S.J. *(China)*

Rev. Paschal LoBianco, S.V.D. *(Ghana)*

Rev. Vincent Loeffler, C.M. *(China)*

Rev. Matt J. Menger, O.M.I. *(Laos)*

Rev. Francis J. O'Neill, M.M. *(China)*

Rev. Ceferino Ruiz, S.J. *(Cuba)*

Rev. Sigfrid Schneider, O.F.M. *(China)*

Rev. Ismael Teste *(Cuba)*

†*Deceased*